THE NEPHILIM AGENDA

THE **NEPHILIM** AGENDA

Exposing the Ultimate Last Days Deception

RANDY DEMAIN

Copyright © 2010 – Randy DeMain

All rights reserved. This book is protected by the copyright laws of the United States of America. No part of this publication may be reproduced, stored in a retrieval system or transmitted in any form or by any means – electronic, mechanical, photocopy, recording or any other – except for brief quotations, without the prior permission of the author.

Unless otherwise indicated, all Scripture quotations are taken from the New King James Version of the Bible®. Copyright ©1982 by Thomas Nelson, Inc. used by permission. All rights reserved.

Scripture marked (NRSV) is taken from the New Revised Standard Version Bible, copyright 1989, Division of Christian Education of the National Council of the Churches of Christ in the United States of America. Used by permission. All rights reserved.

Published by XP Publishing
A department of Christian Services Association
P.O. Box 1017
Maricopa, Arizona 85139
Unites States of America
www.XPpublishing.com

Printed in Canada

ISBN 13: 978-1-936101-17-7
ISBN 10: 1-936101-17-3

THE REVELATION

THE AGENDA

The Nephilim are positioning themselves to rule the world in degrees of wickedness such as man has never known.

They are infiltrating and establishing beachheads in realms of church, government, media, and economic institutions, where they can influence and control those in power and authority with high-level satanic agendas.

They are extremely evil and relentless.

GOD'S PLAN

God has already secured the victory for His people in the midst of this uprising.

A new breed of consecrated, mighty, Spirit-filled warriors are being prepared by the Spirit of God. They will emerge in this hour.

This company of holy champions will eventually with Christ their King conquer and possess every dimension of influence in the earth. They will fully conquer the Nephilim.

QUESTIONS

Who are the Nephilim?

Who are the consecrated holy ones who will conquer, possess and occupy?

How will the Nephilim be overcome?

Read on!
Find out!

CONTENTS

Foreword	Gwen Shaw	9
Introduction		13
Chapter 1	The Seed War	15
Chapter 2	Angels that Did not Keep their Proper Domain	27
Chapter 3	Nephilim Offspring	43
Chapter 4	Post-Flood Resurgence	57
Chapter 5	Nephilim in Holy Garb	75
Chapter 6	Where Do Demons Come from?	91
Chapter 7	The Mystery of Iniquity	103
Chapter 8	As It Was in the Days of Noah	115
Chapter 9	The Bride without Spot or Wrinkle	131
Chapter 10	Preparing for the Days Ahead	143
Appendix A	Sixteen Strongmen	153
Appendix B	Profile of a False Prophet and other False Ministries and Ministers	160
Appendix C	Names of Nephilim after the Flood	165

FOREWORD

Randy DeMain is one of this generation's courageous writers who has dared to give us the truth, even though it has cost him and his family a price. But then, truth is always very costly. In fact, Truth has been known to have been crucified – and that, by the religious leaders of His day!

Thank you, Randy, for daring to tell us the truth which has been hidden from us for thousands of years. But the hour has come for truth to be revealed. When the prophet Daniel asked the angel of the Lord about the Last Days, he was told by the angel, "Daniel, shut up the words, and seal the book" (Daniel 12:4), and it was repeated to him again, "The words are closed up and sealed till the time of the end" (Daniel 12:9). I like the way it is written in *The Message*, "The message is confidential and under lock and key until the end, until things are about to be wrapped up. The populace will be washed clean and made like new. But the wicked will just keep on being wicked, without a clue about what is happening. Those who live wisely and well will understand what's going on" (Daniel 12:9-10).

God began to reveal end-time secrets when the Holy Spirit was poured out at the beginning of the last century. And every decade since then, more wonderful seals are being opened by the angels, until we come to the full knowledge of the truths which have been hidden from us for so long.

For centuries the Bible was as forbidden to Christians by the church leaders as it is forbidden in Communist, Moslem, and some pagan lands today. Men died cruel deaths to give us the Bible. My forefathers were banished from their homes and countries because they refused to give up their Bibles which had been smuggled into Austria in wine casks. They lived in caves and holes dug in the ground for many years, suffering terrible deprivation, until Russia took them in.

Men have paid a terrible price for every revelation from God. Abraham did, Isaac did, Joseph did, the major and minor prophets did, King David did, and the apostles of Christ did. Even Paul was terribly persecuted by the religious leaders of his day, who worked together with governmental authorities to destroy his testimony of the truths of heaven.

The giants have arrived! They never really left us. But we didn't know just who they were or where they came from. The fallen angels were not destroyed in the flood because they were not made in God's image. They are spirits, and spirits cannot cease to exist.

The giants returned later, as we read of them when the children of Israel came into the Promised Land, and 400 years later when David killed Goliath. The Nephilim were born as a result of the fallen angels violating the daughters of man, thereby producing "hybrids" who became giants in stature (Genesis 6:1-4). They were crossbreeds of fallen spirits and humans. Because they were fathered by these spirits who have no blood – and life is in the blood

FOREWORD

and DNA comes from the father – they could not be redeemed like mortal man, for man is redeemed by the blood of Christ, who was slain for the sinful blood of Adam's race.

DeMain explains who "sired" this hybrid race – not created by God – under God's eternal plan of the ages.

This book will shake you; it will wake you up; it will open your eyes. And you may find the answer to some unanswered questions you have had for a long time, which even the learned have not been able to solve.

You may not agree with all you read, but you will never forget it!

Gwen R. Shaw, Th.D., D.D.

Founder and President of End-Time Handmaidens and Servants Ministry

INTRODUCTION

In 2006, I was sitting in downtown Jerusalem having lunch with my friends, Paul Keith Davis and Peter Nash. The environment was so rich; everywhere we looked seemed to bring a Scripture to mind. We were seated in a partially outdoor setting looking toward the corner of the street. I couldn't help noticing the name of the street was Rephaim Avenue. This only put fuel on the fire as Paul Keith and I had been talking about fallen angels, Cain, and other topics for some time.

Here we were in Jerusalem, close to the Valley of Rephaim where David fought the battle to retake Jerusalem. I began to research this topic much more after my return home. About two years later, Paul Keith published an excellent audio series, "As In the Days of Noah." It seemed this topic wouldn't be silenced, as if the Lord was telling us, among others, to keep this issue alive.

What you have before you is an entry-level introduction into the role of fallen angels and their offspring, the Nephilim. It is conservative in its presentation in hopes others will be provoked to search out more insight to publish in the days ahead. Enjoy!

Randy DeMain

CHAPTER 1

THE SEED WAR

"Do not be deceived." This was the first thing Jesus said to His disciples after they questioned Him about the signs of His coming and the end of days. This same warning was brought forth by His apostles throughout the New Testament, and rightly so.

The third being we are introduced to after the creation account in the book of Genesis is a talking serpent set on usurping the position God gave to man. The serpent's tool? Deception.

The author of the deception that brought about the fall of man is planning another intrusion into planet earth. The magnitude of this coming deception will be strong enough to draw millions of souls into his clutches. Even multitudes of professing Christians will be seduced away from the faith to worship Satan as if he were God.

As astounding as this may sound, it has been foretold in Scripture. World events over the course of human history have been preparing mankind to believe Satan's ultimate deception. I invite you to walk with me through the pages of Scripture that record little-understood events, events that have set the stage for the Nephilim agenda – the revealing of the lawless one who can deceive even the elect, if that were possible.

GOD MADE US TO BE LIKE HIMSELF

Man was created with spiritual intuition – a desire and capacity for the supernatural. Born-again believers, as vessels of the Holy Spirit, are being spiritually transformed by the power of God. They are being conformed into the image of Christ Jesus. Romans 8:28-30 says:

> And we know that all things work together for good to those who love God, to those who are the called according to His purpose. For whom He foreknew, He also predestined to be conformed to the image of His Son, that He might be the firstborn among many brethren. Moreover whom He predestined, these He also called; whom He called, these He also justified; and whom He justified, these He also glorified.

The point of the present and coming deception is to corrupt this process of transformation. Satan does not want anyone to progress from a justified state to a glorified state.

Our desire to become like God, by virtue of a loving relationship with Him, is the place of exploitation by the deceiver. Gaining an understanding of how this deception will come is an advantage for us in the days ahead. Overcoming all the schemes of the enemy is our glorious victory in Christ Jesus!

In creation, God made us as much as possible in His image and likeness. He stopped short of giving us the unlimited knowledge, power and presence that He alone possesses, yet made us to rule and reign with Him over all the world. So stunning is our position before God, the writer of the eighth Psalm declares:

"Yet you have made them a little lower than God, and crowned them with glory and honor" (Psalm 8:5 NRSV). The writer of Hebrews picks up this theme again, giving us a before and after picture of the fall of man:

> For He has not put the world to come, of which we speak, in subjection to angels. But one testified in a certain place, saying: "What is man that You are mindful of him, Or the son of man that You take care of him? You have made him a little lower than the angels; You have crowned him with glory and honor, And set him over the works of Your hands. You have put all things in subjection under his feet." For in that He put all in subjection under him, He left nothing that is not put under him. But now we do not yet see all things put under him (Hebrews 2:5-8).

If the translators had been consistent in translating this verse from the Hebrew to Greek, it would have eliminated much confusion and fear.

MAN WAS MADE JUST BELOW GOD

As stated above from the NRSV, the phrase, "Yet you have made them a little lower than God," has been changed in other translations to read, "a little lower than angels." The Hebrew word in Psalms translated as "God" is *Elohim*, which means consistently "God." For some reason the translators choose to give in to non-Jewish texts and tradition to replace *Elohim* with the Greek word *aggelos* meaning "angels."

This bashful rendering could lead one to believe angels are above and superior to mankind, and that we should fear them. This is exactly what Satan's hordes would like us to believe and practice. Redeemed man is not lower than the angels, rather just below God. The truth is redeemed mankind outranks all order of created beings by Christ Jesus. God has not put the present world or the world to come in subjection to angels, but rather to redeemed mankind.

Follow along with me for a moment as we look more closely at the text in Hebrews chapter two. Verse 7 begins: "You have made him a little lower than the angels," referring to how God made man. Many of us, myself included, related this to creation, concluding that God created us a little lower than angels. The truth is the Hebrew and even the Greek words for *created* have nothing to do with the word *made*. Create carries the idea of "forming, shaping, bringing forth" (see Strong's #2936). The word *made* means "to make less, inferior, to decrease."

When you add the meaning of the phrase "made him a little lower" together with "Elohim, God," it would come out something like this: "Mankind's arm of strength was reduced for a short period of time." Mankind was not created inferior; he was made that way temporarily by God's judgment after his sin in the Garden. This lesser state of existence was met by God's grace and redemption. God restored man's dominion over all things through the Seed of Abraham. He once again crowned him with glory and honor, setting him over the works of God's hands, putting all things in subjection under his feet.

Yet the restoration was not yet complete. The last part of Hebrews 2:8 says, "But now we do not yet see all things put under him." This is speaking of all that Adam lost in his failure, in particular everything under the curse of the earth, including the subsequent need for restoration of man's authority over all the power of the enemy.

THE SEED WAR

WE ARE MADE TO OVERCOME

It seems this is where many believers live in their faith: Saved by grace, but not an overcomer. They live a suspended life of hope for a better future. Rise up, hopeful one, we haven't finished! Look at verse nine:

> But we see Jesus, who was made a little lower than the angels, for the suffering of death crowned with glory and honor, that He, by the grace of God, might taste death for everyone (Hebrews 2:9).

We see Jesus, our overcoming King! He was "made" like us, not created inferior. He was made like us to overcome for us; He suffered and tasted death for everyone. He was also crowned with glory and honor. Having disarmed principalities and powers (Colossians 2:15), He restored our position with God, our authority and power, not just in the earth but also over devils and demons, death and the grave. In effect, Jesus made Satan lower, restoring our spiritual heritage and dominion over him. Jesus was the true first fruits, the Firstborn from the dead. Now we, as His Spirit-filled followers, overcome as He did, ready to reverse the curse!

Psalm 115:16 says, "The heaven, even the heavens, are the Lord's; but the earth He has given to the children of men." From this perspective of man's estate with God, it becomes clear why the devil would want to corrupt man's glorious standing with the Lord. Losing his place as co-ruler of the universe to mankind is the ultimate poetic justice of God. Satan wants to regain his lost status, and even more, he wants to rule the universe and be worshipped as God. He is ready to exploit once again, on a global level, man's desire to know God and be like Him.

THE ORIGIN OF DECEPTION

Let's revisit for a moment the origin and essence of deception to get a good grasp on it for the chapters ahead.

In a covert encounter with Eve, Satan made a play at recovering his lost paradise. He moved upon Eve in the very same iniquity that caused him to sin – exploiting her desire to be like God – touching her spiritual intuition to possess forbidden knowledge. Genesis 3:1-7 says:

> Now the serpent was more cunning than any beast of the field which the Lord God had made. And he said to the woman, "Has God indeed said, 'You shall not eat of every tree of the garden'?" And the woman said to the serpent, "We may eat the fruit of the trees of the garden; but of the fruit of the tree which is in the midst of the garden, God has said, 'You shall not eat it, nor shall you touch it, lest you die.'" Then the serpent said to the woman, "You will not surely die. For God knows that in the day you eat of it your eyes will be opened, and you will be like God, knowing good and evil." So when the woman saw that the tree was good for food, that it was pleasant to the eyes, and a tree desirable to make one wise, she took of its fruit and ate. She also gave to her husband with her, and he ate. Then the eyes of both of them were opened, and they knew that they were naked; and they sewed fig leaves together and made themselves coverings."

DID GOD SAY?

Every downfall of man has occurred when the Word of God was brought into question, resulting in disobedience. "Has God indeed said?" This tactic sounds familiar, doesn't it? In the trial of Jesus in the wilderness, did not Satan call God's Word into question, "If you are the Son of God..." (Luke 4:3).

We are all proud of Eve's first response as she articulates the Word of God back to the crafty serpent (Genesis 3:2-3). But her resolve was short lived. The serpent convinced her there would be no consequence of death for eating the forbidden fruit. She's brought in to the lie, *No death? Hmmm...? Go on ... I'm listening.*

YOU WILL BE LIKE GOD

Then the serpent sets the hook of iniquity in her heart. It becomes overpowering as he speaks:

> "For God knows that in the day you eat of it your eyes will be opened, and you will be like God, knowing good and evil." So when the woman saw that the tree was good for food, that it was pleasant to the eyes, and a tree desirable to make one wise, she took of its fruit and ate. She also gave to her husband with her, and he ate (Genesis 3:5-6).

There it is ... "Your eyes will be opened, and *you will be like God*, knowing good and evil."

The rest is experiential history for all mankind. Satan, having usurped their rule by making them rule breakers, regained a measure of rule. Now through the hearts of mankind, his rulership is increased to the degree disobedience prevails. That day, Satan put in play the "mystery of iniquity," that which Scripture defines as lawlessness. It now comes at man on three fronts described by John the apostle:

> Do not love the world or the things in the world. If anyone loves the world, the love of the Father is not in him. For all that is in the world—the lust of the flesh, the lust of the eyes,

and the pride of life—is not of the Father but is of the world (1 John 2:15-16).

God's Judgment and the Seed Wars

What transpired next is the underlying current in this book: the beginning of the seed wars. After hearing Adam and Eve's version of events leading up to the consumption of the forbidden fruit, God makes a judgment and issues decrees against the serpent, the woman, and the man.

The Serpent's Judgment

So the Lord God said to the serpent: "Because you have done this, you are cursed more than all cattle, and more than every beast of the field; On your belly you shall go, and you shall eat dust all the days of your life. And I will put enmity between you and the woman, and between your seed and her Seed; He shall bruise your head, and you shall bruise His heel" (Genesis 3:14-15).

The Woman's Judgment

To the woman He said: "I will greatly multiply your sorrow and your conception; in pain you shall bring forth children; your desire shall be for your husband, and he shall rule over you" (Genesis 3:16).   4:7

Adam's Judgment

Then to Adam He said, "Because you have heeded the voice of your wife, and have eaten from the tree of which I commanded you, saying, 'You shall not eat of it': "Cursed is the ground for your sake; in toil you shall eat of it all the days of

THE SEED WAR

your life. Both thorns and thistles it shall bring forth for you, and you shall eat the herb of the field. In the sweat of your face you shall eat bread till you return to the ground, for out of it you were taken; for dust you are, and to dust you shall return" (Genesis 3:17-19).

Who Is Going to Rule?

Each listened to the painful results of their acts, as everyone was held accountable for their sin. However, these judgments did not negate the fact Satan had regained a measure of rulership on the earth through the heart of sinful man. It was this newly recovered rulership that God declared war against.

And I will put enmity between you and the woman, and between your seed and her Seed; He shall bruise your head, and you shall bruise His heel" (Genesis 3:15).

This verse identifies a distinct change in life as Adam and Eve knew it. No longer would everyone live to worship and fellowship with God. Now another seed would begin to oppose God through the seed of women. From this time forward the seed wars would begin; enmity between the serpent's seed and her Seed would commence.

For the sake of clarity in the following pages, *serpent seed* refers to all human or hybrid seed (we'll learn about hybrid seed in the following chapters) that works in cooperation with Satan against God. *Her Seed* or the *Promised Seed* refers to the seed of Abraham, the seed of David, and the complete line as established in the first chapter of Matthew to identify the prophesied Messianic line from which Jesus Christ would come.

The promise and prophecy set forth here is that the Seed of woman would someday crush the serpent's head, and that woman in particular would have a part in undoing the effects of the fall. In the fullest sense this speaks of Christ Jesus, who trampled Satan at the cross. It also speaks of those who are in Christ and their ultimate triumph over the evil one (Colossians 2:15; Revelation 12:11).

THE SEED WARS BEGIN

From this decree of the Lord, Satan knew a Savior was forthcoming from the Seed of woman. This Seed would bring about his demise. He must not let this Seed find its root or purpose, so he set in motion the next stage of his plan to corrupt the heart of man. In his fallen state, man's heart was now much more susceptible to iniquity. Satan would begin to increase and perpetuate his role through deceptive allegiances to corrupt or kill the Promised Seed.

Adam and Eve's firstborn was Cain. Satan, Adam and Eve may have thought that Cain was the savior God spoke of – for Adam and Eve, the one to restore them to the paradise of God – for Satan, the one who could bruise his head. That old serpent moved quickly to set the hook with Cain to disqualify him from savior stature and separate him from the presence of God.

It wasn't long before Adam and Eve realized Cain wasn't their savior, but rather a disciple of the serpent's seed. They watched as he took on the attributes of lying, murder, and deception.

In the course of time, Cain and Abel brought their offering to the Lord. It appears Cain brought to the Lord what he considered good enough for God. Abel brought the Lord what He required. Fire fell on Abel's sacrifice, indicating acceptance. No fire fell on Cain's offering.

(This happens over and over in the lives of believers. Many bring to God what they have determined is good enough, yet no fire falls upon the altar of their heart. They become cold and

24

indifferent to God, sin lies at their door, and it becomes more difficult to do what's right. Others, like Abel, gladly seek the Lord, bringing themselves as a living sacrifice, holy and acceptable to the Lord. God's fire falls on their hearts, kindling a flame of passion for the Lord. A lack of fire in a Christian's life is a good indicator they have fallen into a routine void of relationship. They begin to offer God what they have determined is good enough for God. When this happens they begin to take on a religious spirit and go the way of Cain.)

When Satan observed no fire falling on Cain's offering, he moved quickly upon Cain's emotions, stirring up the lawlessness in his heart. Knowing fully he was not the savior, he moved Cain to kill Abel, the Promised Seed.

When God confronted Cain, he wasn't sorry for what he did; he was only sorry he got caught. When God offered him a way of repentance, he rejected it, choosing rather the sin lying at his door. Cain chose to become separated from God and align himself with the curse of Satan.

In this act, we see clearly the first manifestations of the serpent seed in action:

- Deceiving Abel, inviting him into the field under false pretense
- Premeditated murder
- Lying to God about his brother's whereabouts

The apostle John doesn't mince words about Cain's works or chosen identity:

"Not as Cain *who* was of the wicked one and murdered his brother. And why did he murder him? Because his works were evil and his brother's righteous" (1 John 3:12).

In the next chapter, we will continue to see the expansion of the serpent's seed as it seeks to destroy the Promised Seed. The stage is set for the first wave of fallen angels to set themselves up as gods while the godly line of Seth arises to keep the Promised Seed alive!

CHAPTER 2

ANGELS THAT DID NOT KEEP THEIR PROPER DOMAIN

After the murder of Abel, God drove Cain out of His presence to wander the earth as a vagabond and fugitive. In defiance of God's decree, Cain decided not to wander, but rather settle in the land of Nod on the east side of Eden. There he took a wife of unknown origin and built a city after the name of his firstborn son, Enoch. (This is not the Enoch that was taken up by the Lord. This is his evil cousin, son of Cain. Cain and his sons began to populate the earth with their wicked offspring, perpetuating evil on every side.)

Evil Grows on the Earth

Methushael, the third from Enoch, was the first to be called a Canaanite, the mixed nation of people who would become the embodiment of every evil and wicked desire of Satan (see Genesis 4:18).

Evil began to be disbursed throughout the earth by the vagabond lifestyle of Cain's sons, Irad, Mehujael, and Methushael. The land

THE NEPHILIM AGENDA

was cursed to them, so they began to hunt and kill, taking what they wanted, be it man, woman, or beast. Their reputation was well established.

Next in the line of Cain comes Lamech. He was bold and defiant in the face of God. He was a polygamist and cold-blooded killer. Lamech had three sons by his two wives: Jabal, Jubal, and Tubal-Cain.

Lamech's wives must have been unique women because the Scripture records their names, as well as Tubal-Cain's sister, Naamah. When a woman's name is recorded in genealogies, it is for one of two reasons: they are virtuous or they are evil and to be avoided. Knowing that Cain wasn't listed as a son in Adam's genealogy (Genesis 5:1-3), but rather under the Toledot (Jewish Torah reading) of the history of the heavens and earth, I think it's safe to say something out of the ordinary was going on and these women were not desirable in God's plan. This far down the road past Adam, it's possible Adah and Zillah were of the corrupted serpent seed. To them, Lamech makes a blasphemous announcement:

> Then Lamech said to his wives: "Adah and Zillah, hear my voice; Wives of Lamech, listen to my speech! For I have killed a man for wounding me, Even a young man for hurting me. If Cain shall be avenged sevenfold, Then Lamech seventy-sevenfold" (Genesis 4:23-24).

Lamech declared he was greater than Cain in his wickedness. He even killed a young man over a minor injury. It seems evil had multiplied in intensity seventy-seven fold.

Jabal and Jubal continued to move about in their cursed vagabond lifestyle. They began to introduce a perversion of music, idolatry, and animal sacrifice in defiance to God. Tubal-Cain,

28

ANGELS THAT DID NOT KEEP THEIR PROPER DOMAIN

whose name means "Flowing like his father," doesn't leave much to our imaginations. Not only was he a liar, murderer, and con artist, he was also an instructor of every craftsman in bronze and iron. As one of the first metal smiths, he began to teach weaponry, crafting arms for war and dominance.

As we shall see just ahead, these last three sons who became skillful in music, medicine, animal husbandry, and metals did not gain these skills on their own. These skills and many others came by the help of angelic visitors.

NEW HOPE IS BORN

God had not forgotten His judgment against Satan, that the Seed would bruise his head. While Cain was populating the earth with the serpent's seed, God was faithfully bringing forth His Promised Seed through the line of Seth. After a hundred and thirty years of mourning, Adam and Eve rejoiced at the arrival of a new baby boy.

> And Adam knew his wife again, and she bore a son and named him Seth, "For God has appointed another seed for me instead of Abel, whom Cain killed" (Genesis 4:25).

At last, now the godly Seed from whom the Messiah would come had arrived on the scene.

A PROPHETIC MESSAGE

From the genealogy of Seth, we can understand what was going on during the time of Cain. God used the names of Seth's offspring to reveal their failure at stopping the insurgence of the serpent seed through the line of Cain, and pinpointing major events of satanic intrusions along the way. The similarity of the names of Cain and Seth's sons and grandsons is amazing. The name of Cain's sons frame the negative works of darkness, the name of Seth's progeny speaks of God's intentions during their time.

In biblical times, parents would name their children according to what they believed to be their life's message and purpose. Their name was inclusive of their destiny. For example, we see God speaking to them through the meaning of the names of Adam and his sons:

Adam: Man
Seth: Appointed
Enosh: Mortal
Cain: Sorrow
Mahalelel: The blessed glorious God
Jared: Shall come down (descended)
Enoch: Teaching (initiated)
Methuselah: His death shall bring
Lamech: The despairing (wild man)
Noah: Rest and comfort

Paul Keith Davis first made this pattern known to me. It is startling when the definitions of their names are read as a sentence:

Man appointed moral sorrow, the blessed God shall come down teaching. His death shall bring the despairing comfort and rest.

God was preaching the gospel of the Messiah through the names of the Promised Seed!

If you take that understanding further, God was prophesying a major event that would transpire at the end of Methuselah's life. His life was watched closely because of the meaning of his name. Methuselah comes from the words Meth and shalak – Meth meaning

ANGELS THAT DID NOT KEEP THEIR PROPER DOMAIN

"to die," and *shalak* meaning "to send forth." The meaning is clear: at his death, judgment shall be sent forth.

What judgment was to come forth? It was the flooding of the earth in Noah's lifetime that would destroy all flesh on the earth.

THE FIRST PROFANING OF THE NAME OF THE LORD

One might wonder why it would be necessary to destroy all flesh. Seth was a good guy. Enoch pleased God; He took him alive to live forever in heaven with him. What was going on that was corrupting the good seed?

The answer can be found by discovering what transpired around the time of Enosh and Jared. God chose to reveal the infiltration of evil that occurred, not so much because of them, but rather on their watch. Let's begin with Seth's firstborn, Enosh:

> And as for Seth, to him also a son was born; and he named him Enosh. Then men began to call on the name of the Lord" (Genesis 4:26).

This verse can easily be misunderstood at face value. It sounds as though everything has come back into right order. Cain and his bunch have gone off after their endeavors and now men begin to call on the name of the Lord. Unfortunately, just the opposite is true. The godly are getting caught up in the way of Cain, allowing mixture into their lives. Consider this insight from E. W. Bullinger's Appendix Number 21 from the Companion Bible:

> Enos. (Gen 4:26.) "CALLING ON THE NAME OF THE LORD."[1]

---

[1] The Companion Bible, Appendix 21 by E. W. Bullinger originally published 1922, no copyright.

"Then began men to call upon the name of Jehovah." If this refers to Divine worship it is not true: for Abel and Cain both began, and their descendants doubtless followed their example.

What was really begun was the profanation of the Name of Jehovah. They began to call something by the Name of Jehovah. The A.V. suggests: "themselves" in the margin. But the majority of the ancient Jewish commentators supply the Ellipsis by the words "their gods"; suggesting that they called the stars and idols their gods, and worshipped them.

The Targum of Onkelos explains it: "then in his days the sons of men desisted from praying in the Name of the Lord."

The Targum of Jonathan says: "That was the generation in whose days they began to err, and to make themselves idols, and surnamed their idols by the Name of the Word of the Lord."

Kimchi, Rashi, and other ancient Jewish commentators agree with this. Rashi says: "Then was there profanation in calling on the Name of the Lord."

Jerome says that this was the opinion of many Jews in his days.

Maimonides, in his Commentary on the Mishna (a constituent part of the Talmud), A.D. 1168, in a long treatise on idolatry, gives the most probable account of the origin of idolatry in the days of Enos.

The name Enos agrees with this, for his name means frail, weak, sickly, incurable. The sons of men, as "Enosh", are so called for a similar reason (Job 7:17; 15:14; Psalm 9:20; 103:15; Daniel 2:43). See Appendix 14 of The Companion Bible.

ANGELS THAT DID NOT KEEP THEIR PROPER DOMAIN

If Jonathan, the grandson of Moses, became the first idolatrous priest in Israel (see notes on Judges 18:30 in The Companion Bible), what wonder that Enos, the grandson of Adam, introduced idolatry among mankind.

Moreover, what "ungodliness" did Enoch, "the seventh from Adam" have to prophesy about in Jude 14-15 if purity of worship was begun in the days of Enos, instead of profanation in calling on the Name of the Lord?

Surely this is sufficient evidence that this profanation of the Name of the Lord was the reason why Enoch was raised up to prophesy against it."

THE USE OF HISTORICAL TEXTS

To help us understand what began to transpire on the earth from this time forward, resulting in the flood, I will be utilizing several historical texts. These texts, known as apocryphal and pseudepigraphical writings, are still included in a number of Bible translations, but no longer recognized as Canon. Many of these texts were found among the Scriptures recovered from Qumran cave systems containing the Dead Sea scrolls. These scrolls were sacred to the people at that time. Many of them are quoted from or made reference to in the Bible. The book of Enoch in particular was memorized by Jesus and the disciples as Canon. It wasn't removed from Scripture until the Council of Constantinople in 553 A.D. The Council determined First and Second Peter, Jude, and Enoch among others, were too explicit for the common mind to engage. First and Second Peter and Jude survived the Council. Enoch and other works were ordered destroyed, being labeled heretical, expanding earlier anti-Jewish trends that were put forth in 327 A.D.

This act is just one of many efforts that have occurred in church history to dumb down believers and take away a true understanding of the supernatural aspect of our lives.

To be clear, I am not saying these ancient writings carry the weight of Scripture, but rather am pointing out that they offer valuable historical information. To be sure, the Bible is my complete source of truth whereby everything else is measured. I use these ancient texts much like I use word studies, commentaries, or a lexicon. These texts provide light on obscure events or definitions that otherwise leave one to much mental conjecture and uncertainty.

Watcher Angels Chosen to Instruct Godly Seed

Enosh, or Enos, was born approximately 3769 B.C., 230 some years after Adam. We know from biblical texts that the practice of idolatry was introduced in his time as the result of corrupt angelic interaction. Let's look back in history and observe the events that led up to this practice.

And in the second week of the tenth jubilee Mahalalel took unto him to wife Dinah, the daughter of Barakiel the daughter of his father's brother, and she bare him a son in the third week in sixth year, and he called his name Jared, for in his days the angels of the Lord descended on the earth, those who are named the Watchers, that they should instruct the children of men, and that they should do judgment and uprightness on the earth.[2]

With the proliferation of evil spreading across the earth through the serpent seed, those who were of the Promised Seed needed instruction from the Lord. In the absence of the Holy

---

[2] Jubilees 4:15; www.sheepkillers.com/giantsnephilim.html; 9/4/2009

34

ANGELS THAT DID NOT KEEP THEIR PROPER DOMAIN

Spirit, who was not yet present upon man, and being removed from the presence of the Lord in the Garden, God chose watcher angels to instruct the Promised Seed.

We are familiar with watcher angels from Daniel's account of them (Daniel 4:13, 17, 23). They are interactive with the affairs of men.

The watchers that came in the days of Enos to teach righteousness and justice quickly became perverted as evidenced by the idolatry among them. Men began worshipping these angelic beings by making replicas of them and calling them by the name of the Lord.

WATCHER ANGELS FALL INTO CORRUPTION

Now Satan could take his game of corruption and deception to a whole new level. The watcher angels saw that the daughters of men were beautiful, and desired them. This was Satan's opportunity to strike:

> And it came to pass when the children of men had multiplied that in those days were born unto them beautiful and comely daughters. And the angels, the children of the heaven, saw and lusted after them, and said to one another: "Come, let us choose us wives from among the children of men and beget us children." And Semjaza, who was their leader, said unto them: "I fear ye will not indeed agree to do this deed, and I alone shall have to pay the penalty of a great sin." And they all answered him and said: "Let us all swear an oath, and all bind ourselves by mutual imprecations not to abandon this plan but to do this thing." Then sware they all together and bound themselves by mutual imprecations upon it. And they were in all two hundred; who descended in the days of Jared on the summit of Mount Hermon, and

they called it Mount Hermon, because they had sworn and bound themselves by mutual imprecations upon it. And these are the names of their leaders: Samlazaz, their leader, Araklba, Rameel, Kokablel, Tamlel, Ramlel, Danel, Ezeqeel, Baraqijal, Asael, Armaros, Batarel, Ananel, Zaqiel, Samsapeel, Satarel, Turel, Jomjael, Sariel. These are their chiefs of tens (Enoch 6:1-8).

Twenty leaders of ten bound themselves by mutual imprecations to leave their heavenly habitation permanently to be joined to human women. This happened in the days of Jared, who was born approximately 225 years after Enos.

What you are about to read next will assault every sense of human morality and dignity one has. Your mental capacity will be stretched and your theology strained:

And all the others together with them took unto themselves wives, and each chose for himself one, and they began to go in unto them and to defile themselves with them, and they taught them charms and enchantments, and the cutting of roots, and made them acquainted with plants. And they became pregnant, and they bare great giants, whose height was three thousand ells: Who consumed all the acquisitions of men. And when men could no longer sustain them, the giants turned against them and devoured mankind. And they began to sin against birds, and beasts, and reptiles, and fish, and to devour one another's flesh, and drink the blood. Then the earth laid accusation against the lawless ones (Enoch 7:1-6).

These rebellious angels set in motion the vilest wickedness ever known to mankind. Watcher angels, who can take on human form [yes, we entertain some of them unaware (Hebrews 13:2)], began to

ANGELS THAT DID NOT KEEP THEIR PROPER DOMAIN

manipulate human and animal DNA, mixing terrestrial flesh with celestial flesh.

> But God gives it a body as He pleases, and to each seed its own body. All flesh is not the same flesh, but there is one kind of flesh of men, another flesh of animals, another of fish, and another of birds. There are also celestial bodies and terrestrial bodies; but the glory of the celestial is one, and the glory of the terrestrial is another (1 Corinthians 15:38-40).

This going after strange flesh was outright rebellion against God, as we know from Levitical law recorded in chapters eighteen and nineteen of Leviticus:

> "You shall not uncover the nakedness of a woman and her daughter, nor shall you take her son's daughter or her daughter's daughter, to uncover her nakedness. They are near of kin to her. It is wickedness.... You shall not lie with a male as with a woman. It is an abomination. Nor shall you mate with any animal, to defile yourself with it. Nor shall any woman stand before an animal to mate with it. It is perversion. Do not defile yourselves with any of these things; for by all these the nations are defiled, which I am casting out before you. For the land is defiled; therefore I visit the punishment of its iniquity upon it, and the land vomits out its inhabitants" (Leviticus 18:17, 22-25).

> "You shall keep My statutes. You shall not let your livestock breed with another kind. You shall not sow your field with mixed seed. Nor shall a garment of mixed linen and wool come upon you" (Leviticus 19:19).

The moral corruption and manipulation of every species of plant and animal was occurring. Every sort of idolatry, perversion, and wicked practice imaginable began to fill the earth. Murder, rape, incest, and cannibalism were common. Part human, part animal creatures began to appear. Giant men and giant crops – like the single cluster of grapes Moses' spies returned with – were in the earth. Homosexuality, witchcraft, and Satanism were brought to their highest levels as the fallen watchers began to bring corruption of creative knowledge to men in exchange for their daughters.

Structural Advancements Begin to Occur

It is interesting to note that it was also in this time that mounds, buildings, and structures such as the Egyptian pyramids began to appear all over the earth. Great advances – some that exceed what we know today in science, medicine, astronomy, and engineering – came into the earth. These things would be consistent with this era considering what the watchers taught:

> And Azazel taught men to make swords, and knives, and shields, and breastplates, and made known to them the metals of the earth and the art of working them, and bracelets, and ornaments, and the use of antimony, and the beautifying of the eyelids, and all kinds of costly stones, and all colouring tinctures. And there arose much godlessness, and they committed fornication, and they were led astray, and became corrupt in all their ways. Semjaza taught enchantments, and root-cuttings, Armaros the resolving of enchantments, Baraqijal (taught) astrology, Kokabel the constellations, Ezeqeel the knowledge of the clouds, Araqiel the signs of the earth, Shamsiel the signs of the sun, and Sariel the course of the moon. And as men perished, they cried, and their cry went up to heaven" (Enoch 8:1-3).[3]

---

[3] Charles, R. H. *The Book of Enoch* 8:1-3, pgs 18-20. Escondido, California: The Book Tree © 1999.

ANGELS THAT DID NOT KEEP THEIR PROPER DOMAIN

And their judges and rulers went to the daughters of men and took their wives by force from their husbands according to their choice, and the sons of men in those days took from the cattle of the earth, the beasts of the field and the fowls of the air, and taught the mixture of animals of one species with the other, in order therewith to provoke the Lord; and God saw the whole earth and it was corrupt, for all flesh had corrupted its ways upon earth, all men and all animals (Jasher 4:18).[4]

The book of Jasher was familiar to the Old Testament writers; it is referenced in Joshua 10:12-13 and 2 Samuel 1:18. Jasher chapter 4 contains much of the same information as Genesis chapter 5. It records the downward spiral of degradation of mankind.

GOD'S CREATION IS CORRUPTED AND EXPLOITED

Hundreds of years of unchecked lawlessness has by now invaded the earth. Every aspect of God's creation has been corrupted and exploited. The renegade angels have ravished the earth and its inhabitants. The serpent seed seems to be prevailing over the Promised Seed. If the Promised Seed can be corrupted, Satan will have prevailed and the earth would be his. By now, all the faithful fathers have died, their children, with the exception of a few, have gotten caught up in the corruption. In this darkest moment, when it seems all is about to be lost, Enoch brings some good news:

And then Michael, Uriel, Raphael, and Gabriel looked down from heaven and saw much blood being shed upon the earth, and all lawlessness being wrought upon the earth. And they said one to another: "The earth made without inhabitant cries the voice of their cryingst up to the gates of heaven. And now to you, the holy ones of heaven, the souls

---

[4] http://www.sacred-texts.com/chr/app/jasher/4.htm 1/20/2009

of men make their suit, saying, 'Bring our cause before the Most High.'" And they said to the Lord of the ages: "Lord of lords, God of gods, King of kings, and God of the ages, the throne of Thy glory (standeth) unto all the generations of the ages, and Thy name holy and glorious and blessed unto all the ages! Thou hast made all things, and power over all things hast Thou: and all things are naked and open in Thy sight, and Thou seest all things, and nothing can hide itself from Thee. Thou seest what Azazel hath done, who hath taught all unrighteousness on earth and revealed the eternal secrets which were (preserved) in heaven, which men were striving to learn: And Semjaza, to whom Thou hast given authority to bear rule over his associates. And they have gone to the daughters of men upon the earth, and have slept with the women, and have defiled themselves, and revealed to them all kinds of sins. And the women have borne giants, and the whole earth has thereby been filled with blood and unrighteousness. And now, behold, the souls of those who have died are crying and making their suit to the gates of heaven, and their lamentations have ascended: and cannot cease because of the lawless deeds which are wrought on the earth. And Thou knowest all things before they come to pass, and Thou seest these things and Thou dost suffer them, and Thou dost not say to us what we are to do to them in regard to these" (Enoch 9:1-11).[5]

The tipping point had been reached and the souls of men began to cry out to God. The archangels had also been taking notice and brought the matter before the Lord Most High. The Lord instructed the holy angels of God to tell Lamech's son Noah to get ready!

---

[5]Charles, R. H. *The Book of Enoch 9:1-11*, pgs 20-22. Escondido, California: The Book Tree © 1999

ANGELS THAT DID NOT KEEP THEIR PROPER DOMAIN

Then said the Most High, the Holy and Great One spake, and sent Uriel to the son of Lamech, and said to him: "Go to Noah and tell him in my name 'Hide thyself!' and reveal to him the end that is approaching: that the whole earth will be destroyed, and a deluge is about to come upon the whole earth, and will destroy all that is on it. And now instruct him that he may escape and his seed may be preserved for all the generations of the world" (Enoch 10:1-4).[6]

After this excursion through Scripture, now it's easier to understand why God set out to destroy all flesh!

All had become defiled, altered, and corrupt. The existing world was no longer of God's creation; it was the serpent's seed desecration. Elohim, The Most High Creator God, true to His Word, is about to step in to annihilate this wickedness and preserve the Promised Seed.

---

[6]Charles, R. H. *The Book of Enoch* 10:1-4, pgs 13-16. Escondido, California: The Book Tree © 1999.

CHAPTER 3

NEPHILIM OFFSPRING

The biblical account of what transpired from the time of Enos is recorded in Genesis 6. With the view from the historical books of Enoch and Jasher in place, now let's take a look at what the Bible has to say:

> Now it came to pass, when men began to multiply on the face of the earth, and daughters were born to them, that the sons of God saw the daughters of men, that they *were* beautiful; and they took wives for themselves of all whom they chose. And the Lord said, "My Spirit shall not strive with man forever, for he *is* indeed flesh; yet his days shall be one hundred and twenty years." There were giants on the earth in those days, and also afterward, when the sons of God came in to the daughters of men and they bore *children* to them. Those *were* the mighty men who *were* of old, men of renown (Genesis 6:1-4).

Who were the "sons of God" that saw the daughters of men were beautiful? We know what the historical books say. They reveal their identity as fallen watcher angels who were part of Satan's rebellion. Let's take a close look at the text here in Genesis 6 and see if this is indeed the case.

Let's begin by establishing who the daughters of men are. They are ... yes, you guessed it ... the daughters of men. The correct conclusion is that they were simply fully human females.

Who Were the "Sons of God"?

It is the identity of the "sons of God" that has been the subject of debate for some time. It appears to me that their identity is quite clear; however, others see things differently. Decide what you think. Here are the three predominate views:

1. **Fallen watcher angels.** This view receives the greatest criticism because it goes against all collective human reason. Further, it seems to contradict what Jesus said about angels neither marrying or being given in marriage in Matthew 22:30: "For in the resurrection they neither marry nor are given in marriage, but are like angels of God in heaven."

2. **Male descendants of Seth.** This view embraces the identity of the sons of God as being the direct bloodline of Seth who marry the corrupt daughters of Cain.

3. **Men of nobility.** This view is held mainly by Orthodox Jews.

Now let's break down these views beginning with numbers two and three, then work back to number one.

Men of Nobility and Descendants of Seth Views

With all due respect to those who have set forth these views, numbers two and three fail to explain the atrocities that came upon the earth resulting in its destruction by the judgment of God. While numbers two and three satisfy our humanity and logic, they do not explain the vile wickedness or the race of giants that came from their union.

Nowhere in the history of humanity has God wiped out all flesh from the face of the earth because of mixed marriages of humans. Furthermore, there is no record of godly men and ungodly women producing the offspring of Titans, giants or half-human, half-animal beings. The offspring of the union between the sons of God and the daughters of men were not ordinary humans. As we will see shortly, these were massive giants between nine and thirteen feet tall, conservatively speaking. Some had six fingers and six toes. They were cannibalistic, lustful beings without conscience. The historical writings tell us Adam and his line stopped having children, knowing judgment was pending. The men of nobility were nowhere to be found; all had become vile. The men of renown that the Genesis account speaks of were not noble. These men were renowned for their fierceness and for their insatiable appetites of violence, lust and perversion. These also could not have been the offspring of the godly line of Seth; Genesis 6:5 declares they were all wicked.

Fallen Watcher Angels View

A look into the original Hebrew reveals the sons of God were no less than fallen angels, the teraphim class of angels that can take on a human form for extended periods of time. They were not permitted to marry in heaven where the perfect will of God is lived, but in their rebellion, they did marry on earth.

The Hebrew renders the sons of God as *B'nai Ha Elohim*. The Strong's concordance renders it simply Strong's #1121 plus Strong's #430 *Ben Elohiym*: son of God. This terminology is always used of angels in the Old Testament, never of men. It only appears four times, and each time it refers to angels.

The "Sons of God" in the Old Testament

Job 38:4-7 says: "Where were you when I laid the foundations of the earth? Tell *Me*, if you have understanding. Who determined its measurements? Surely you know! Or who stretched the line upon it? To what were its foundations fastened? Or who laid its cornerstone, When the morning stars sang together, And all the sons of God shouted for joy?" Only angels were present at the foundation of the earth, and in particular on the third day when this event took place. Man was not created until the sixth day.

The book of Job also describes two times when Satan and the "sons of God" came before the Lord:

> Now there was a day when the sons of God came to present themselves before the Lord, and Satan also came among them (Job 1:6).

> Again there was a day when the sons of God came to present themselves before the Lord, and Satan came also among them to present himself before the Lord (Job 2:1).

Among the sons is Satan, who himself is a cherub angel, thus again making the identity of the "sons of God" angelic.

The other account is in Daniel, speaking of the fourth man in the fire, who is identified as one "like the Son of God" again referring to a supernatural being (see Daniel 3:25).

It seems clear to me that the "sons of God" who saw the daughters of men were angels.

This is reinforced by the Hebrew word, "iyr," defined in the Gesenius Hebrew lexicon #5894 as "watcher" in the identification of the watcher angels Daniel observed in Daniel 4:13, 17.

The Sons of God are Watcher Angels

We can further identify these sons of God as a class of angels called Teraphim. The account of Rachel stealing the household idols from her father is a window we can look through to establish this identity.

> Now Rachel had taken the household idols, put them in the camel's saddle, and sat on them. And Laban searched all about the tent but did not find *them* (Genesis 31:34).

The household idols Rachel took were images of fallen watcher angels. The words *image* and *idol* are interchangeable in this passage. The Hebrew word translated here is the word *teraphiym* meaning "healer, oracle, one who watches over." These idols were venerated as powerful oracles able to provide salvation, guidance and protection. Through these mediums the fallen watchers and demonic spirits spoke and acted.

This provides additional proof of the identity of the sons of God as being watcher angels, and also helps explain the idolatry behind the spiritually charged images and figures worshipped in the pre-flood era.

> And Uriel said to me: "Here shall stand the angels who have connected themselves with women, and their spirits assuming many different forms are defiling mankind and shall lead them astray into sacrificing to demons as gods, (here shall they stand,) till the day of the great judgment in which they shall be judged till they are made an end of" (Enoch 19:1-2).[7]

The apostle Peter informs us that angels sinned and were cast out of heaven (2 Peter 2:4). Jude tells us some of these angels did

---

[7] Charles, R. H. *The Book of Enoch* 19:1-2, pgs 42-43. Escondido, California: The Book Tree © 1999.

not keep their proper domain, but gave themselves over to sexual immorality and went after strange flesh (Jude 1:6-7). This seems to me to be ample evidence of the identity of the sons of God and their corrupt activities. Activities were so grossly inhumane and wicked, God pronounced this judgment:

> Then the Lord saw that the wickedness of man was great in the earth, and *that* every intent of the thoughts of his heart *was* only evil continually. And the Lord was sorry that He had made man on the earth, and He was grieved in His heart. So the Lord said, "I will destroy man whom I have created from the face of the earth, both man and beast, creeping thing and birds of the air, for I am sorry that I have made them" (Genesis 6:5-7).

THE OFFSPRING OF THE SONS OF GOD

At this point, I want to introduce you to the offspring of the union between the sons of God and the daughters of men. It is these beings that Satan will use in the future, just as he did in the days of Noah, to attempt to derail the plan of God and corrupt the seed of man. Most translations refer to them as giants; their formal name is Nephilim.

The Nephilim are a hybrid race of part human, part angelic origin. They are the corruption of the serpent seed, altered from God's designed creation.

They are the mixture of terrestrial flesh and celestial flesh. They are the reason God had to destroy the earth by a flood. They are the reason the children of Israel were instructed to kill every man, woman and child in their land of inheritance; they had been defiled and corrupted by the serpent seed, the Nephilim.

NEPHILIM OFFSPRING

There were giants on the earth in those days, and also afterward, when the sons of God came in to the daughters of men and they bore *children* to them. Those *were* the mighty men who *were* of old, men of renown" (Genesis 6:4).

The word translated "giants" is Nephilim, meaning "fallen one" (from *naphal* Strong's #5303, to fall).

These offspring of the fallen angels have other alarming meanings attached to their name. *Nephilim* from the root Niphal means "distinguished ones." The Hebrew consonants "npl" as found in Psalm 58:8 means "miscarriage" and "to speak control over life." The Strong's concordance traces Nephilim as "a living abortion"; a ghost-like power.

However you look at it, the Nephilim were not good. These Nephilim, the hybrid offspring of angels and human women, were known as mighty (Strong's #1368 *gibbowr*), giant, powerful, warring tyrants.

Some of the more famous Nephilim are Goliath (who David killed) and Og, King of Bashan (1 Samuel 17:4-6; Deuteronomy 3:11). The sons of these giants are called Rephaim, from the Hebrew word *Rapha*, Strong's #7497. From these come a host of offspring by other names we will discuss later.

The Nephilim were the avatar of the fallen watcher angels. In the Webster's New Dictionary, *Avatar* means: 1. Hinduism: a god coming to earth in a bodily form. 2. An embodiment as of a quality of a person.[8] The Bible calls them the men of renown or the men of old.

THE DESTRUCTION OF THE NEPHILIM THROUGH THE FLOOD

The Nephilim corrupted man and beast, plant life, and fish to the point that God said, "Every intent of the thoughts of his heart (the heart of man) was only evil continually" (Genesis 6:5).

[8] Webster's New Dictionary: Copyright 2003 by Wiley Pub.

So the Lord said, "I will destroy man whom I have created from the face of the earth, both man and beast, creeping thing and birds of the air, for I am sorry that I have made them" (Genesis 6:7).

THE NEPHILIM ASK FOR MERCY

The events that transpired at the time of the flood were swift and decisive. The historical accounts tell us that the original group of fallen watchers asked Enoch to intercede on their behalf before God after the Lord gave Gabriel instructions to destroy the children of the fallen watchers.

And to Gabriel said the Lord: "Proceed against the bastards and the reprobates, and against the children of fornication: and destroy [the children of fornication and] the children of the Watchers from amongst men [and cause them to go forth]: send them one against the other that they may destroy each other in battle: for length of days shall they not have" (Enoch 10:9-10).

And I Enoch was blessing the Lord of majesty and the King of the ages, and lo! the Watchers called me –Enoch the scribe– and said to me: "Enoch, thou scribe of righteousness, go, declare to the Watchers of the heaven who have left the high heaven, the holy eternal place, and have defiled themselves with women, and have done as the children of earth do, and have taken unto themselves wives: 'Ye have wrought great destruction on the earth: And ye shall have no peace nor forgiveness of sin: and inasmuch as they delight themselves in their children, The murder of their beloved ones shall they see, and over the destruction of their children shall they lament, and shall make supplication unto eternity, but mercy and peace shall ye not attain.'"

And Enoch went and said: "Azazel, thou shalt have no peace: a severe sentence has gone forth against thee to put thee in bonds: And thou shalt not have toleration nor request granted to thee, because of the unrighteousness which thou hast taught, and because of all the works of godlessness and unrighteousness and sin which thou hast shown to men." Then I went and spoke to them all together, and they were all afraid, and fear and trembling seized them. And they besought me to draw up a petition for them that they might find forgiveness, and to read their petition in the presence of the Lord of heaven. For from thenceforward they could not speak (with Him) nor lift up their eyes to heaven for shame of their sins for which they had been condemned (Enoch 12:3-13:6).

Enoch Brought the Fallen Watchers' Petition Before God

Having overstayed their time on earth, they had become earthbound. Enoch went on their behalf and returned with this answer from God Most High:

I wrote out your petition, and in my vision it appeared thus, that your petition will not be granted unto you throughout all the days of eternity, and that judgment has been finally passed upon you: yea (your petition) will not be granted unto you. And from henceforth you shall not ascend into heaven unto all eternity, and in bonds of the earth the decree has gone forth to bind you for all the days of the world. And (that) previously you shall have seen the destruction of your beloved sons and ye shall have no pleasure in them, but they shall fall before you by the sword. And your petition on their behalf shall not be granted, nor yet on your own: even though you weep and pray and speak all the words contained in the writing which I have written" (Enoch 14:4-8).

The Watchers' Petition Was Not Granted

The Nephilim and their offspring were doomed forever:

> And the Lord said unto Michael: "Go, bind Semjaza and his associates who have united themselves with women so as to have defiled themselves with them in all their uncleanness. And when their sons have slain one another, and they have seen the destruction of their beloved ones, bind them fast for seventy generations in the valleys of the earth, till the day of their judgment and of their consummation, till the judgment that is for ever and ever is consummated. In those days they shall be led off to the abyss of fire: and to the torment and the prison in which they shall be confined for ever. And whosoever shall be condemned and destroyed will from thenceforth be bound together with them to the end of all generations. And destroy all the spirits of the reprobate and the children of the Watchers, because they have wronged mankind" (Enoch 10:11-15).[9]

The watchers had been sentenced as well as their offspring. The fallen watchers were to be bound in the abyss, their offspring to be killed by the sword and the coming deluge. They were granted no forgiveness or repentance even though they sought for it with tears.

Jude agrees with these historical accounts:

> But I want to remind you, though you once knew this, that the Lord, having saved the people out of the land of Egypt, afterward destroyed those who did not believe. And the angels who did not keep their proper domain, but left their own abode, He has reserved in everlasting chains under darkness for the judgment of the great day; as Sodom and

---

[9]Charles, R. H. *The Book of Enoch* 10:11-15, pgs 24-25. Escondido, California: The Book Tree © 1999.

Gomorrah, and the cities around them in a similar manner to these, having given themselves over to sexual immorality and gone after strange flesh, are set forth as an example, suffering the vengeance of eternal fire (Jude 1:5-7).

JUDGMENT AGAINST THE FALLEN WATCHER ANGELS

Prior to the ark's voyage, God began His first wave of judgment against the 200 rebel angels who left their first estate. Jude tells us they were "reserved in everlasting chains under darkness" (verse 6).

This imprisonment occurred after their offspring killed one another by the sword. Now confined to eternal destruction, they await their final sentence (Revelation 20:10; Matthew 25:41).

This prison of darkness is the dreaded place of all evil spirits. According to Scripture, it is the deepest, darkest place in the abyss known as Tartarus, the place the fallen watchers, among others, are currently chained.

So frightful is this place, the demons that were in the Gaderene demoniac pleaded with Jesus not to send them there (Mark 5). This place hasn't seen its last action. When the fifth angel sounds his trumpet, this pit will be opened to release its inhabitants upon the earth again.

> Then the fifth angel sounded: And I saw a star fallen from heaven to the earth. To him was given the key to the bottomless pit. And he opened the bottomless pit, and smoke arose out of the pit like the smoke of a great furnace. So the sun and the air were darkened because of the smoke of the pit (Revelation 9:1-2).

The verses that follow describe that out of this smoking furnace will come locust-type creatures who will sting people but not kill them. Their leader is named Abbadon in Hebrew, and in Greek, Apollyon, which means destroyer.

The Nephilim that did not kill each other with the sword lost their host bodies in the flood. These became disembodied spirits confined to the earth and under the earth by the judgment of God.

Isaiah 26:14 makes it clear that these shall not find forgiveness or resurrection to eternal life (also see John 8:23-24). However, unlike their parents who were chained in Tartarus, these Nephilim spirits remain loose to seduce and corrupt mankind until the consummation of all things.

(As for the spirits of heaven, in heaven shall be their dwelling, but as for the spirits of the earth which were born upon the earth, on the earth shall be their dwelling.) And the spirits of the giants afflict, oppress, destroy, attack, do battle, and work destruction on the earth, and cause trouble: they take no food, but nevertheless hunger and thirst, and cause offences. And these spirits shall rise up against the children of men and against the women, because they have proceeded from them. From the days of the slaughter and destruction and death of the giants, from the souls of whose flesh the spirits, having gone forth, shall destroy without incurring judgment – thus shall they destroy until the day of the consummation, the great judgment in which the age shall be consummated, over the Watchers and the godless, yea, shall be wholly consummated (Enoch 15:10-16:2).[10]

JESUS PROCLAIMED HIS VICTORY TO THE SPIRITS IN PRISON

To the fallen angels and those bound to the earth, Jesus came and proclaimed to them their final and eternal defeat.

---

[10] Charles, R. H. *The Book of Enoch* 15:10-16:2, pg 36-37. Escondido, California: The Book Tree © 1999.

For Christ also suffered once for sins, the just for the unjust, that He might bring us to God, being put to death in the flesh but made alive by the Spirit, by whom also He went and preached to the spirits in prison, who formerly were disobedient, when once the Divine longsuffering waited in the days of Noah, while *the* ark was being prepared, in which a few, that is, eight souls, were saved through water" (1 Peter 3:18-20).

The apostle Peter tells us the same Spirit that raised Christ from the dead took Him to Tartarus to preach to the spirits in prison. While many have suggested that Jesus went to preach to the lost souls of men, this would be incomplete within the context of "Noah" in the passage. Also, the word *preach* to many means to evangelize rather than to simply "proclaim," as it does in this passage. Furthermore, the word *spirits* always refers to divine beings unless otherwise specified. And finally, the Gospel is for men, not angels.

The Scripture is clear that men do not get a second chance or marinate their way to heaven from a holding place. Jesus went to proclaim to the spirits in prison His victory over the fallen ones – His victory at the cross that sealed the judgment over them. He went from the lowest place to begin His declaration, to the highest place at the right hand of God. Colossians 2:15 declares that Jesus "disarmed principalities and powers, [and] He made a public spectacle of them, triumphing over them in it." So complete and everlasting is His victory that, from that moment on, the prophesy of Isaiah 53 was fulfilled.

Jesus ascended from hell's lowest place to heaven's highest place, leading a victorious parade of the righteous, those once held in Sheol until the victory was won. What a glorious day! A day that forever changed the authority and power structure of the spirit world. The triumphant Son of God had now regained what man had lost.

The Flood Was Effective

The flood was 100 percent effective. It destroyed all flesh from the face of the earth, except that which was aboard the ark. Now the purposes of God could be restored upon the earth. Righteous Noah and his family, who successfully held off Nephilim contamination, would surely continue in their uprightness. The earth would be healed and restored now that the watchers are chained in the deepest darkest hell and the Nephilim had no flesh to live in. The righteous Seed had prevailed. Conclusion: It must be time to plant a vineyard and celebrate!

And Also Afterward...

This sounds like a movie with a happy ending, one you leave and feel good inside. Then, just at the last moment, that which you thought was dead ... isn't. So it is with the Nephilim. Remember the haunting phrase from Genesis 6:4, "And also afterward"?

> There were giants on the earth in those days, and also afterward, when the sons of God came in to the daughters of men and they bore *children* to them. Those *were* the mighty men who *were* of old, men of renown (Genesis 6:4).

A resurgence occurred after the flood, for the Nephilim were on the earth *after* the flood, just like *before*.

Noah, you have some explaining to do!

CHAPTER 4

POST-FLOOD RESURGENCE

I am constantly amazed at God's unwavering hope in mankind – that we will arise and live as overcomers in this world. Equally amazing is that He oftentimes seems to place the future of His program in the hands of a single individual. So, like many of you, I am ever moving toward being such an individual God could single out, knowing He could count on me to do the right thing. Let not the words of Ezekiel be heard on our watch:

> So I sought for a man among them who would make a wall, and stand in the gap before Me on behalf of the land, that I should not destroy it; but I found no one (Ezekiel 22:30).

In the midst of the unraveling account of the seed wars, God brings to our attention one we admire. An individual we could see ourselves being like under similar circumstances. Noah stands out in the bleak darkness like an aircraft landing beacon. God had made up His mind; He was sorry He had made man. Now He was going to have to destroy all flesh from the earth, all, that is, except one. There was one who had not disappointed His hope. Noah found grace in the eyes of the Lord. The holy habitation of heaven must have sung gloriously when God found him.

For over 1,600 years, wickedness increased upon the earth from Adam's first breath in 4004 B.C. until the flood around 2348 B.C. The mystery of iniquity had successfully corrupted nearly every living thing. It is difficult to grasp the propensity of mankind to align themselves to works of darkness. This propensity leaves no doubt in my mind that sin is nothing to toy around with. Unbelief, rebellion, seemingly little acts of sinfulness are evidence that we have an appetite for lawlessness.

If you are like me, I say with all my heart, "Away with you, Satan, and all your wicked devils and demons, I will have nothing to do with you! I will not carry any evidence of your presence or influence in my life. I am the Lord's and His alone. You will not bring any corruption or destruction to this earth or mankind through my actions or thoughts!"

It's good to say such things out loud every so often, and state your stance and purpose of business.

Noah Walked With God

Noah took everything the fallen watchers and their offspring threw at him and remained untainted. Be encouraged when it seems everyone else has gone the way of Cain; God is looking for those who will remain faithful. God is looking for those He can bestow grace on to overcome. Consider the account of Noah:

> This is the genealogy of Noah. Noah was a just man, perfect in his generations. Noah walked with God. And Noah begot three sons: Shem, Ham, and Japheth. The earth also was corrupt before God, and the earth was filled with violence. So God looked upon the earth, and indeed it was corrupt; for

all flesh had corrupted their way on the earth. And God said to Noah, "The end of all flesh has come before Me, for the earth is filled with violence through them; and behold, I will destroy them with the earth. Make yourself an ark of gopherwood; make rooms in the ark, and cover it inside and outside with pitch" (Genesis 6:9-14).

How did Noah keep his way in the midst of great wickedness?

Verse 9 tells us he learned an overcoming way of life from his great, great, great grandpa Enoch. Like Enoch, Noah walked with God.

This relationship with the Lord kept Noah, a just man, perfect in his generations. The word *perfect* doesn't mean morally perfect in this verse. The Hebrew word used – *tamim* – carries the meaning "to be without spot or blemish or deformity." In other words, Noah had not taken part in the mingling of himself with the fallen watchers. Therefore, Noah was an untainted carrier of the Seed of Promise, one who could continue the lineage of the Messiah.

The Promised Messiah Would Come Through Noah's Seed

It was now through Noah and his family the continuance of the Promised Seed would come forth – the Messiah who would bruise the head of Satan. God said to Noah:

> "And behold, I Myself am bringing floodwaters on the earth, to destroy from under heaven all flesh in which *is* the breath of life; everything that *is* on the earth shall die. But I will establish My covenant with you; and you shall go into the ark— you, your sons, your wife, and your sons' wives with you" (Genesis 6:17-18).

God said, "Noah, you have remained faithful to me, therefore, I will make my covenant with you. Through you and your family, I will re-start the earth and repopulate its entirety though you." One can almost hear Noah's mind processing the implications of God's grace and mercy. This is the reality of a holy life. God was staking the future of the human race on Noah to live for God after the flood like he did before the flood. To bring forth on the earth a holy gene pool from which the Messiah would come forth.

Right on schedule, the rains came down, and the fountains under the earth opened up. Noah, his family and the animals God brought to him rested safely above while all flesh was destroyed below. So complete was God's judgment against evil, the reinstated covenant with Noah was void of the command to subdue the earth and have dominion. Nothing and no one was left.

> "Bring out with you every living thing of all flesh that *is* with you: birds and cattle and every creeping thing that creeps on the earth, so that they may abound on the earth, and be fruitful and multiply on the earth." Then Noah built an altar to the Lord, and took of every clean animal and of every clean bird, and offered burnt offerings on the altar. And the Lord smelled a soothing aroma. Then the Lord said in His heart, "I will never again curse the ground for man's sake, although the imagination of man's heart *is* evil from his youth; nor will I again destroy every living thing as I have done" (Genesis 8:17, 20-21).

The economy of earth, the innocence of creation had now changed. The fear of man would now be in all the beasts, birds and marine life. All things were now given as food sources for mankind. Within this covenant, God put in place a system of laws that would protect man and animal from the former abuses. No longer could

60

POST-FLOOD RESURGENCE

unchecked bloodshed run rampant without judgment and punishment brought upon the lawless one.

> "And the fear of you and the dread of you shall be on every beast of the earth, on every bird of the air, on all that move on the earth, and on all the fish of the sea. They are given into your hand. Every moving thing that lives shall be food for you. I have given you all things, even as the green herbs. But you shall not eat flesh with its life, *that is*, its blood. Surely for your lifeblood I will demand *a reckoning*; from the hand of every beast I will require it, and from the hand of man. From the hand of every man's brother I will require the life of man. Whoever sheds man's blood, By man his blood shall be shed; For in the image of God He made man. And as for you, be fruitful and multiply; Bring forth abundantly in the earth And multiply in it" (Genesis 9:2-7).

NOAH GETS DRUNK AND THE DOOR OPENS AGAIN

And now, just when it seems all is well in the world, Noah does the unthinkable. Noah got drunk! This was all Satan needed to gain access into the Promised Seed and turn the battle back to his favor. Instead of winning the war, the flood was just another battle. Now the Nephilim would have a new host soul, a way in to regroup and start again with their corruptive ways.

> And Noah began *to be* a farmer, and he planted a vineyard. Then he drank of the wine and was drunk, and became uncovered in his tent. And Ham, the father of Canaan, saw the nakedness of his father, and told his two brothers outside. But Shem and Japheth took a garment, laid *it* on both their shoulders, and went backward and covered the nakedness of their father. Their faces *were* turned away, and they did not

see their father's nakedness. So Noah awoke from his wine, and knew what his younger son had done to him. Then he said: "Cursed *be* Canaan; A servant of servants he shall be to his brethren" (Genesis 9:20-25).

"Cursed be Canaan." Observing the incapacitated state of Noah, now Ham does the unthinkable. He opens the door to the most desirable acts of the roaming Nephilim: sexual perversion. Some suggest Ham had homosexual relations with his father Noah. This can be deducted by observing the activities of the offspring of Canaan, particularly as seen in Sodom and Gomorrah. Others understand "uncovering his father's nakedness" implies he engaged in sexual relationship with his mother. Regardless, it is evident some type of sexual misconduct took place.

The Scriptures say that as a man thinks in his heart, so is he, and out of the abundance, the fullness of the heart, the mouth speaks (See Proverbs 4:23; Matthew 12:34-35; 15:18).

Jesus also made it very clear that if a man lusts after a woman in his heart, he has committed adultery in God's eyes:

> But I say to you that whoever looks at a woman to lust for her has already committed adultery with her in his heart (Matthew 5:28).

It is clear a second intrusion of fallen watcher took place somewhere before Genesis chapter 14. My personal opinion is that it occurred here. It seems quite possible that Ham got caught up in a moment of lust, establishing a doorway for a spirit of lust to enter him and use his body to carry out shameful acts.

Once embodied, Ham had no means of deliverance. Therefore his offspring would carry and increase the iniquity of sexual perversion to its fullest capacity.

POST-FLOOD RESURGENCE

Another possibility is that a watcher angel could have come and enticed Ham to come in league with him for dominion, power, and pleasure in the new world. Genesis 9:24 says that when Noah awoke from his wine he knew what his younger son had done to him. This suggests some evidence. There could have been an altar set up to sexual spirits or evidence consistent with sexual activity. Rather than postulate theories, there is a proven method to uncover hidden mysteries.

The best method of detection in cases such as this is to follow the bloodline, follow the seed, to see what kind of fruit it produces.

A simple reading of Genesis 10 is eye opening as one sees the development of the Canaanites, the Philistines, and their principal cities. Each place became a harbinger for Nephilim activity. (See Appendix C for the identification of post-flood Nephilim.)

THE NEPHILIM AGENDA SPREADS THROUGH HAM'S LINE

The cursed line of Ham seemed to wholly give themselves over to the Nephilim agenda. The blessed sons of Noah, Shem and Japheth started well but began a slow downward spiral into idolatry. Abraham became the next bright line down the godly line surfacing in Genesis chapter 12.

Between the time of Noah and Abraham, the giants and tyrants began to appear again. Of particular interest is an up and coming Nephilim King by the name of Nimrod:

> The sons of Ham were Cush, Mizraim, Put, and Canaan. The sons of Cush were Seba, Havilah, Sabtah, Raamah, and Sabtechah; and the sons of Raamah were Sheba and Dedan. Cush begot Nimrod; he began to be a mighty one on the earth. He was a mighty hunter before the Lord; therefore it is said, "Like Nimrod the mighty hunter before the Lord."

And the beginning of his kingdom was Babel, Erech, Accad, and Calneh, in the land of Shinar. From that land he went to Assyria and built Nineveh, Rehoboth Ir, Calah, and Resen between Nineveh and Calah (that *is* the principal city) (Genesis 10:6-12).

From Ham's son, Cush, came forth Nimrod. The Scripture tells us he "began" to be a "mighty one" on the earth. The word *began* indicates a process, a discipline. Nimrod began to be a "mighty one." The word mighty is *ghib-bore* meaning "powerful and by implication a warrior, a tyrant, a chief, a giant mighty man" (Strong's #1368). This is the same word used in Genesis 6:4 to describe the giants, the Nephilim.

Nimrod wasn't a mighty hunter of game, rather the souls of men – souls the disembodied Nephilim could possess. Nimrod began to build cities as places for habitation for wicked and unclean spirits. Together they began to build a tower into the heavenlies providing safety above the flood line and access into heaven, thrones, and dominions for earthbound spirits. Some suggest he became a Nephilim, or at least, a king over the Nephilim. He exchanged the souls of men to them, the Nephilim, for the right to rule over them. Nimrod was obsessed with establishing a kingdom that God could not destroy. He was intent on destroying the Promised Seed.

E.W. Bullinger writes:

Nimrod. Genesis 10:8-9; 1 Chronicles 1:10

Joshephus (Ant. Jud. i. c. 4. 2) says: "Nimrod persuaded mankind not to ascribe their happiness to God, but to think that his own excellency was the source of it. And he soon changed things into a tyranny, thinking there was no other way to wean men from the fear of God than by making them rely upon his own power."

The Targum of Jonathan says: "From the foundation of the world none was ever found like Nimrod, powerful in hunting, and in rebellions against the Lord."

The Jerusalem Targum says: "He was powerful in hunting and in wickedness before the Lord, for he was a hunter of the sons of men, and he said to them, 'Depart from the judgment of the Lord, and adhere to the judgment of Nimrod!' Therefore is it said: 'As Nimrod [is] the strong one, strong in hunting, and in wickedness before the Lord.'"

The Chaldee paraphrase of 1 Chronicles 1:10 says: "Cush begat Nimrod, who began to prevail in wickedness, for he shed innocent blood, and rebelled against Jehovah."

Nimrod was the founder of Babylon, which partook of his character as being the great antagonist of God's Truth and God's People.

We cannot fail to see, in Nimrod, Satan's first attempt to raise up a human universal ruler of men. There have been many subsequent attempts, such as Nebuchadnezzar, Alexander, Napoleon, and others. He will finally succeed in the person of the antichrist.[11]

The Spread of the Nephilim Continues

The spread of the Nephilim after the flood appears to be more concentrated in the Middle East. This may be due to the destruction of the tower of Babel, the confusion of languages, and the fact that in the days of Peleg the earth was divided from a single landmass into its present form.

[11] The Companion Bible, Appendix 28, pg 29, by E. W. Bullinger originally published 1922, no copyright.

The first incursion of the watchers affected the whole planet. An Internet search of "giants" will shock the first time explorer. Every country of the world has uncovered evidence of a race of giants living among normal society. In the United States of America, there are ancient markings in caves by Egyptians and Phoenician travelers dedicating the land to the star gods, Baal in particular. Giant human fossils and graves have been discovered in nearly every state.

The following is from Appendix 25 of the Companion Bible:

...So that "after that," i.e. after the Flood, there was a *second* irruption of these fallen angels, evidently smaller in number and more limited in area, for they were for the most part confined to Canaan, and were in fact known as "the nations of Canaan." It was for the destruction of these, that the sword of Israel was necessary, as the Flood had been before.

As to the date of this second irruption, it was evidently soon after it became known that the Seed was to come through Abraham; for, when he came out from Haran (Genesis 12:6) and entered Canaan, the significant fact is stated: "The Canaanite was then (i.e. *already*) in the land." And in Genesis 14:5 they were already known as "Rephaim" and Emim," and had established themselves at Ashteroth Karnaim and Shaveh Kiriathaim.

In chapters 18-21 of Genesis they are enumerated and named among Canaanite Peoples: "Kenites, and the Kenizzites, and the Kadmonites, and the Hittites, and the Perizzites and the Rephaims, and the Amorites, and the Girgashites, and the Jebusites" (Genesis 15:19-21; cp. Exodus 3:8,17; 23:23; Deuteronomy 7; 20:17; Joshua 12:8).

These were to be cut off, and driven out, and utterly

POST-FLOOD RESURGENCE

destroyed (Deuteronomy 20:17; Joshua 3:10). But Israel failed in this (Joshua 13:13; 15:63; 16:10; 17:18; Judges 1:19-20, 28-29, 30-36; 2:1-5; 3:1-7); and we know not how many got away to other countries to escape the general destruction. If this were recognized, it would go far to solve many problems connected with Anthropology.

As to their other names, they were called Anakim, from one Anak which came of the Nephilim (Numbers 13:22) and Rephaim, from Rapha, another notable one among them.

From Deuteronomy 2:10, they were known by some as Emim, and Hovim, and Zamzummim (verses 20-21) and Avim.

As Rephaim they were well known, and are often mentioned: but, unfortunately, instead of this, their proper name, being preserved, is variously translated as "dead," "deceased," or "giants." These Rephaim are to have no resurrection. This fact is stated in Isaiah 26:14 (where the proper name is rendered "deceased," and verse 19, where it is rendered "the dead").

It is rendered "dead" seven times (Job 26:5; Psalm 88:10; Proverbs 2:18; 9:18; 21:16; Isaiah 14:8; 26:19).

It is rendered "deceased" in Isaiah 26:14.

It is retained as a proper name "Rephaim" ten times (two being in the margin). Genesis 14:5; 15:20; Joshua 12:15 (margin); 2 Samuel 5:18,22; 23:13; 1 Chronicles 11:15; 14:9; 20:4 (margin); Isaiah 17:5.

In all other places it is rendered "giants," Genesis 6:4, Numbers 23:33, where it is gibbor (Ap. 14 iv).

By reading all these passages the Bible student may know all that can be known about these beings.

67

It is certain that the second irruption took place before Genesis 14, for there the Rephaim were mixed up with the five nations or peoples, which included Sodom and Gomorrah, and were defeated by the four kings under Chedorlaomer. Their principal locality was evidently "Ashtaroth Karnaim"; while the Emim were in the plain of Kiriathaim (Genesis 14:5).

Anak was a noted descendant of the Nephilim; and Rapha was another, giving their names respectively to different clans. Anak's father was Arba, the original builder of Hebron (Genesis 35:2; Joshua 15:13; 21:11); and this Palestine branch of the Anakim was not called Arbahim after him, but Anakim after Anak. They were great, mighty, and tall (Deuteronomy 2:10-11, 21-23; 9:2), evidently inspiring the ten spies with great fear (Numbers 13:33). Og king of Bashan is described in Deuteronomy 3:11.[12]

Satan Tries To Destroy the Promised Seed

As soon as it was made known that the Seed of woman was to come through Abraham, the enemy began to fully occupy the land of Canaan in advance of Moses' arrival with the children of Israel. The serpent seed was out to deny entrance in the land of promise.

When Abraham entered Canaan (Genesis 12:6) the Nephilim were already in the land and launched a generational battle to destroy the Promised Seed.

The following is Appendix 23 of The Companion Bible, edited and formatted slightly for easier readability:

---

[12] From The Companion Bible, Appendix 25, pg 28, by E. W. Bullinger originally published 1922, no copyright.

"The Sons of God" in Genesis 6:2,4

It is only by the Divine specific act of creation that any created being can be called "a son of God." For that which is "born of the flesh is flesh." God is spirit, and that which is "born of the Spirit is spirit" (John 3:6). Hence Adam is called a "son of God" (Luke 3:38). Those "in Christ" having "the new nature," which is by the direct creation of God, can be and are called "sons of God" (2 Corinthians 5:17; Ephesians 2:10; John 1:13; Romans 8:14-15; 1 John 3:1).

This is why angels are called "sons of God" in every other place where the expression is used in the Old Testament (Job 1:6; 2:1; 38:7; Psalms 29:1; 89:6; Daniel 3:25). We have no authority or right to take the expression in Genesis 6:2, 4 in any other sense. Moreover, in Genesis 6:2 the Septuagint renders "sons of God" as "angels."

Angels are called "spirits" for spirits are created by God (Psalm 104:4; Hebrews 1:7, 14).

That there was a fall of the angels is certain from Jude 6.

The nature of their fall is clearly stated in the same verse. They left their own (*oiketerion*). This word occurs only in 2 Corinthians 5:2 and Jude 6, where it is used of the spiritual (or resurrection) body.

The nature of their sin is stated to be "in like manner" to that of the subsequent sins of Sodom and Gomorrah (Jude 7).

The time of their fall is given as having taken place "in the days of Noah," though there may have been a prior fall which caused the end of "the world that then was" (1 Peter 3:20; 2 Peter 2:7; Genesis 1:1-2; 2 Peter 3:6).

For this sin they are "reserved unto judgment" and are "in prison" (2 Peter 2:4).

Their progeny, called *Nephilim* (translated "giants"), were monsters of iniquity; and, being superhuman in size and character, had to be destroyed. This was the one and only object of the Flood.

Only Noah and his family had preserved their pedigree pure from Adam (Genesis 6:9). All the rest had become "corrupt." The only remedy was *to destroy it* (*de facto*), as it had become *destroyed* (*de jure*). (It is the same word in verse 17 as in verses 11-12.)

This irruption of fallen angels was Satan's first attempt to prevent the coming of the Seed of the woman foretold in Genesis 3:15. If this could be accomplished, God's Word would have failed, and his own doom would be averted.

As soon as it was made known that the Seed of the woman was to come through *Abraham*, there must have been another irruption, as recorded in Genesis 6:4, "and also after that" (i.e., after the days of Noah, more than 500 years after the first irruption). The aim of the enemy was to occupy Canaan in advance of Abraham, and so to contest its occupation by his seed. For, when Abraham entered Canaan, we read "the Canaanite was then (i.e., already) in the land" (Genesis 12:6).

In the same chapter (Genesis 12:10-20) we see Satan's next attempt to interfere with Abraham's Seed and frustrate the purpose of God that it should be in "Isaac." This attempt was repeated in Genesis 20:1-18.

This great conflict may be seen throughout the Bible, and it forms a great and important subject of biblical study.

POST-FLOOD RESURGENCE

In each case the human instrument had his own personal interest to serve, while Satan had his own great object in view. Hence God had, in each case, to interfere and avert the evil and the danger, of which His servants and people were wholly ignorant. The following assaults of the great Enemy stand out prominently:

- The destruction of the chosen family by famine (Genesis 50:20).
- The destruction of the male line in Israel (Exodus 1:10, 15-16;. Exodus 2:5; Hebrews 11:23).
- The destruction of the whole nation in Pharaoh's pursuit (Exodus 14).
- After David's line was singled out (2 Samuel 7), that was the next one selected for assault. Satan's first assault was in the union of Jehoram and Athaliah by Jehoshaphat, notwithstanding 2 Chronicles 17:1. Jehoram killed off all his brothers (2 Chronicles 21:4).
- The Arabians slew all his children, except Ahaziah (2 Chronicles 21:17; 22:1).
- When Ahaziah died, Athaliah killed "all the seed royal" (2 Chronicles 22:10). The babe Joash alone was rescued; and, for six years, the faithfulness of Jehovah's Word was at stake (2 Chronicles 23:3).
- Hezekiah was childless when a double assault was made by the King of Assyria and the King of Terrors (Isaiah 36-39). God's faithfulness was appealed to and relied on (Psalm 136).
- In Captivity, Haman was used to attempt the destruction of the whole nation (Esther 3:6,12-13. Cp.6:1).

- Joseph's fear was worked on (Matthew 1:18-20). Notwithstanding the fact that he was "a just man," and kept the Law, he did not wish to have Mary stoned to death (Deuteronomy 24:1); hence Joseph determined to divorce her. But God intervened: "Fear not."
- Herod sought the young Child's life (Matthew 2).
- At the Temptation, "Cast Thyself down" was Satan's temptation.
- At Nazareth, again (Luke 4), there was another attempt to cast Him down and destroy Him.
- The two storms on the Lake were other attempts.
- At length the cross was reached, and the sepulcher closed; the watch set; and the stone sealed. But "God raised Him from the dead" And now, like another Joash, He is seated and expecting, hidden in the house of God on high; and the members of "the one body" are hidden there "in Him" (Hebrews 10:12-13; Colossians 3:1-3). Like another Jehoshaba; and going forth to witness of His coming, like another Jehoiada (2 Chronicles 23:3).
- The irruption of "the fallen angels" ("sons of God") was the first attempt; and was directed against the whole human race.
- When Abraham was called, then he and his seed were attacked.
- When David was enthroned, the royal line was assailed.

- And when "the Seed of the woman" Himself came, then the storm burst upon Him.[13]

THE NEPHILIM HIDE THEMSELVES

Account after account in Scripture tells us of Satan's unsuccessful attempts to destroy the Promised Seed that would bruise the head of Satan. Systematically, the Israelites overcame and conquered the Nephilim until they went underground or out of sight (Deuteronomy 3:11; 31:4).

In their existing form, the Nephilim were easy targets. They could not hide in society. After their numbers and cities decreased, they were forced to take on another form to be in position when "her Seed" became flesh. What better disguise than holy garb. The Nephilim are about to shift from bloody tyrants to a place of sophistication that would enable them to convince the people to kill their Messiah. **The plot thickens.**

---

[13] Appendix 23 of The Companion Bible, pg 26, 27 by E. W. Bullinger originally published 1922, no copyright

CHAPTER 5

NEPHILIM IN HOLY GARB

A favorite saying of Senator James E. Watson was, "If you can't lick 'me, jinee 'me." Later it took on a more sophisticated verbiage rendering the modern adage, "If you can't beat them, join them."

This appears to be the stratagem of the next advance of the Nephilim. Their original giant size, in many instances, began to normalize through the generations. This is evidenced by the mixture of the seven-nation compilation of the Canaanites and the five Lords of the Philistines who began to rule on the coast (Joshua 13). Giants did continue in many areas, even through King David's time, but were systematically eliminated to the point of near extinction. Not being able to overcome the Promised Seed outwardly, it was time to infiltrate so as to overcome them from within. Only their appearance changed; their nature and agenda remained the same. The Nephilim began to covertly move into sectors of government, education, finance, and religion. From these positions, they could influence – even control – the masses and accomplish their agenda.

The Judges and Kings of Israel

From the period of the judges of Israel through the reign of their kings, the Nephilim gained strength and position. An overview of the kings reveals an ebb and flow from spiritual high points to the lowest of lows. The spiritual bent of the king determined the spiritual climate of the day.

The dynasty of Omri, King of Israel, did much harm to the Promised Seed. This man placed a welcome mat in front of any doors of wickedness not opened by previous kings. The marriage of his son, Ahab, to the Phoenician princess, Jezebel, ushered in the false prophets of Baal and Asherah, the licentious forms of worship and human sacrifice practiced by the early Sidonians. The Sidonians worshipped the star gods, celestial entities, practiced tantric rituals involving bloodletting and nearly every wicked thing spoken of in Scripture. They were sworn enemies of God's people. The granddaughter of Omri was Athaliah, the daughter of Jezebel. Athaliah was given in marriage to Jehoram as part of Satan's plan to introduce idolatry into Judah, just as Jezebel did in Israel.

The Religious Leaders of Israel

Not as powerful as kings, but equally influential were the Scribes, Pharisees, and priests. A look back at their beginnings was good. They performed an essential role in God's purposes. We discover it wasn't long before the rank and file of these elite were infiltrated. Jonathan is singled out as the first idolatrous priest (Judges 18:30).

Hopi and Phinehas, the sons of Eli, the priest, were present in the days of the kings. The worship of Belial became prominent throughout the culture at that time. The corruption of Eli's sons was over the top. They disregarded the holy things of God. They were greedy gluttons with unchecked sexual appetites. They had become full blown serpent seed. They daily profaned the temple of God and the priesthood.

> Now the sons of Eli *were* corrupt; they did not know the Lord (1 Samuel 2:12).

The literal meaning of the word *corrupt* is "sons of Belial." What is amazing is how close they were able to be to the ark of the covenant and the people of God (1 Samuel 4:4).

Judgment ultimately did come upon the house of Eli and his sons. Hopi and Phinehas were killed while escorting the ark of the covenant into battle. At the news of Hopi and Phinehas' death, Eli fell over and died. Phinehas' wife then died giving birth to a son named Ichabod, meaning "inglorious," for the glory of the Lord had departed from Israel (1 Samuel 4:17-22). In their place, God had raised up a pure and holy priest named Samuel, who would keep wickedness and evil in check throughout his life.

When I was a new Christian, I would read the accounts of the scribes, Pharisees, and Sadducees with great admiration. I thought they were great, holy men of God, and I couldn't reconcile John's blazing comments to them:

> But when he saw many of the Pharisees and Sadducees coming to his baptism, he said to them, "Brood of vipers! Who warned you to flee from the wrath to come?" (Matthew 3:7)

I noticed that Jesus was rather short and blunt with these men as well:

> Brood of vipers! How can you, being evil, speak good things? For out of the abundance of the heart the mouth speaks (Matthew 12:34).

I knew something was up. These were not well-meaning people trying to expose what they thought was a false teacher. These were the stock of the serpent seed who knew exactly who Jesus was. He was the Messiah, the Promised Seed they must destroy before He destroyed them. Once the scribes and Pharisees were sure who He was, they set in motion a smear campaign from their deceptive roles to bring about the demise of the long awaited Anointed One. They would gather false witnesses against Jesus to dismiss Him as a blasphemous man to be crucified, and assure the Israelites that the Messiah was still to come.

When this deception was fully in place, the people would rise up against Jesus and put Him to death. The plan was sure to succeed. The Promised Seed that would bruise the head of Satan would once and for all be destroyed.

Scribes and Pharisees Started Well

Before I grind down these sects of religious leaders any further, let me give credit where credit is due. The early scribes and Pharisees who transmitted the Holy Scriptures to us must be applauded. Before corruption fully set in, they accomplished their duties well.

It is because of them we know the Scriptures are exact, reliable, and true to every letter. They utilized extraordinary means of early checks and balances to transmit the sacred writing to us with utmost accuracy.

An exhortation of one of the Rabbi's solemn warnings to his associates says, "Take heed how you do your work, for your work is the work of heaven, lest you drop or add a letter of the manuscript, and so become the destroyer of the world."

Edomites Infiltrate the Religious Order

After the Assyrian domination of Israel and the Babylonian captivity of Judah, the role of judges and kings came to a close. This created a leadership vacuum for the people of God and established a perfect opportunity for Satan to fully infiltrate the religious order of the day. During the period of Babylonian captivity, the serpent seed would move into the mostly vacated area of Southern Judea. They would be in place upon their return. As the Israelites began to return to rebuild, they found a mixed multitude had settled in. The predominate group were Idumeans, that is, Edomites of the line of Esau, the source of Jacob's trouble.

The Edomites remained somewhat under the radar during the years of Ezra and Nehemiah, although a steady resistance was put forth by them to slow the city-rebuilding project. For about the next 400 years, there was silence. As the area began to grow and the original returning religious order began to die off, the Edomites began a process of assimilation into their roles. It wasn't long before the scribes, Pharisees, and priests were from Edomite decent. In the absence of judges and kings, the respect and popularity of the scribes and Pharisees began to grow. They soon replaced the prophets and priests as father figures for all Israel.

It seems to be a pattern in Scripture of God allowing wickedness to fully ripen before He separates the wheat from the tares.

It was only after the fullness of the iniquity of the Amorites that God brought the children of Israel out of Egypt. It was only after the fullness of the Canaanite wickedness that God sent Israel in to destroy them. Here again it seems God has allowed the Nephilim seed to come into fullness before He sends forth His Son in the fullness of time. Each cycle took about 400 years to reach maturity and experience judgment.

Edomites Infiltrate Civil Government to Murder the Messiah

In 40 B.C., Herod, an Edomite chieftain, conquered Judea to become its king. The Romans recognized his place of authority and made him governor in 37 B.C.

With the civil government in place, now the Edomite scribes and Pharisees could rise to full stature. It's not a surprise that the Scripture declares Herod was terrified by the announcement of Christ's arrival. Satan had positioned him to destroy the Messiah upon arrival.

> Now after Jesus was born in Bethlehem of Judea in the days of Herod the king, behold, wise men from the East came to Jerusalem, saying, "Where is He who has been born King of the Jews? For we have seen His star in the East and have come to worship Him." When Herod the king heard *this*, he was troubled, and all Jerusalem with him (Matthew 2:1-3).

> Then Herod, when he saw that he was deceived by the wise men, was exceedingly angry; and he sent forth and put to death all the male children who were in Bethlehem and in all its districts, from two years old and under, according to the time which he had determined from the wise men (Matthew 2:16).

Herod died in 4 B.C. His successor was his own son, Herod Archelaus. He failed in his role and was replaced by a non-Herodite Jew, Pontius Pilate.

The Offspring of Vipers

With the exception of a few such as Joseph of Arimathea and others who later came to faith, most all other scribes and Pharisees were Edomites that came into position after the Babylonian captivity.

Let's consider why both John and Jesus condemned them and refused their baptism. Jesus said, "Serpents, brood of vipers! How can you escape the condemnation of hell?" (Matthew 23:33).

The term *generation of vipers* means "seed, offspring or brood," indicating their DNA source.

Jesus called them what they were: Nephilim seed, the serpent seed from days of old.

With the voice of the prophets silenced during the previous 400 years, the Nephilim began to distort and complicate the law of God. They made it nearly impossible to acquire redemption by establishing complex rules known as the "Tradition of the Elders." Their voice became law and their tradition began to overshadow the law of God. Jesus said that they made "the word of God of no effect through your tradition which you have handed down. And many such things you do" (Mark 7:13). No wonder Jesus was intolerant of them.

The Scribes and Pharises stood before Jesus, brazenly attempting to prove that their good works and genealogy qualified them as heirs of God's salvation and blessing. In this fifth woe pronounced to them, Jesus systematically exposed them for who they really were: children of their father, the devil, who cannot escape the condemnation of hell (Matthew 23:33).

John didn't mince any words with this group either. In effect he said, "Seed of Satan, who warned you to get out of harm's way?" (Matthew 3:7). Then, he goes a step further to make it clear to them as Enoch did earlier. There is no repentance or salvation for them.

> "And do not think to say to yourselves, 'We have Abraham as *our* father.' For I say to you that God is able to raise up children to Abraham from these stones. And even now the

ax is laid to the root of the trees. Therefore every tree which does not bear good fruit is cut down and thrown into the fire" (Matthew 3:9-10).

John knew this group did not come out to be baptized; they had no intention to humble themselves. These were Edomites in holy garb. If they thought that declaring they were the seed of Abraham might save them, they were wrong!

In a similar encounter, Jesus backs up John's profiling and brings clarity to the seed issue.

"I know that you are Abraham's descendants, but you seek to kill Me, because My word has no place in you. I speak what I have seen with My Father, and you do what you have seen with your father" (John 8:37-38).

Apparently this wasn't clear enough for them and they begin to exchange words about parentage and works. Finally Jesus' bottom lines it for them, leaving them no response except to accuse Him of having a demon and then attempting to stone Him.

"Why do you not understand My speech? Because you are not able to listen to My word. You are of *your* father the devil, and the desires of your father you want to do. He was a murderer from the beginning, and does not stand in the truth, because there is no truth in him. When he speaks a lie, he speaks from his own *resources*, for he is a liar and the father of it" (John 8:43-44).

While it was true they were descendants of Abraham, it was equally true they were from the wrong branch. They were descendants of Ishmael, of Esau, of the corrupted Edomites, sworn enemies of God.

Now this brood had come to the fullness of time. God was about to bring judgment upon the false sons and extend adoption and redemption to the true sons (Galatians 4:3-5). In His eight woes to the scribes and Pharisees, Jesus declared this wicked seed line had been working against the Lord and His anointed for centuries.

The wickedness of the Nephilim had once again reached maturity through the scribes and Pharisees. The Lord would save the true sons from among them and bring swift justice to the rest.

In almost poetic justice, God redeemed Saul, renamed Paul, from their midst to establish a new church government of apostles, prophets, evangelists, pastors, and teachers. He – not the old Order – would write a majority of the New Testament and lay the foundation for the Church.

Judas Iscariot - One of the Twelve

Before we close out this chapter, there is one more provocative character to look at – the one who worked with the Chief Priest, scribes and Pharisees to bring Christ to the cross: the infamous Judas Iscariot.

Judas' last name is not found in any known language. It is believed to represent the malignant nature of the Hebrew word *Ish Kerioth* meaning "a man from Kerioth." In Christ's time, Kerioth was a small village in the southwest part of Judea, the central territory occupied by the Edomites. Judas was an Edomite, a multigenerational avatar of the Nephilim seed. Like Esau, and those after him, he found not repentance for his dastardly deed.

Why would Jesus choose Judas if He knew he was going to betray Him? In speaking to a large crowd of disciples, Jesus spoke to them and said:

"But there are some of you who do not believe." For Jesus knew from the beginning who they were who did not believe, and who would betray Him (John 6:64).

It seems clear that Jesus wants to draw a distinction between those who would believe, and those who under no circumstance would believe. In other words, Satan has some children of his own. Children of wrath, doomed for destruction. These are not simply unbelievers, but are of their father, the devil, set on the destruction of Christ and all who are His.

"For certain men have crept in unnoticed, who long ago were marked out for this condemnation, ungodly men, who turn the grace of our God into lewdness and deny the only Lord God and our Lord Jesus Christ" (Jude 4).

Judas is an example of such men: Individuals who can be among true believers, looking and acting like a Christian, but with evil intentions.

Jesus answered them, "Did I not choose you, the twelve, and one of you is a devil?" He spoke of Judas Iscariot, *the son* of Simon, for it was he who would betray Him, being one of the twelve (John 6:70-71).

In a number of translations and the original Greek, the word *devil* is the Greek word *diabolos* (Strong's #1228). It is consistently translated, "devil." The Greek meaning is to be a traducer, slanderer, false accuser. It appears 38 times in the New Testament, most often describing the identity of the prince of demons or evil spirits present in human activity (Matthew 4:1; Revelation 12:9).

Was Jesus identifying Judas as a Nephilim in disguise, or just a misguided man?

Jesus' strong statement suggests Judas was much more than just a misguided man.

John 12:4 tells us Judas was intending to work within his seed line to betray Jesus, and the gospels point out he was an unscrupulous man and a thief, all the while working signs, wonders, and miracles. During the last supper, Jesus begins to reveal the origins of Judas' kind.

> "I do not speak concerning all of you. I know whom I have chosen; but that the Scripture may be fulfilled, '*He who eats bread with Me has lifted up his heel against Me.*' Now I tell you before it comes, that when it does come to pass, you may believe that I am *He*" (John 13:18-19).

Jesus declares to His disciples one of the most convincing truths to His identity as the Messiah, the Promised Seed. He is saying, "Come on boys, I want you to see this clearly," drawing them to familiar words spoken thousands of years ago:

"He who eats bread with Me has lifted up his heel against Me" (John 13:18).

The disciples' minds may have first gone to the book of Psalms:

"All who hate me whisper together against me; Against me they devise my hurt. 'An evil disease,' *they say*, 'clings to him. And *now* that he lies down, he will rise up no more.' Even my own familiar friend in whom I trusted, Who ate my bread, Has lifted up *his* heel against me" (Psalm 41:7-9).

I picture Jesus allowing the disciples a moment to process, then with a look or gesture indicating they ought to think back even further – all the way to the beginning. Then they may have recalled the Genesis account; it's familiar, but seems out of order:

And I will put enmity between you and the woman, And between your seed and her Seed; He shall bruise your head, And you shall bruise His heel" (Genesis 3:15).

Jesus is saying,

"See how the devil has twisted the Scriptures to make me look like the evil one? He makes himself out to be God. He appears to lift up his heel as bruised, rather than being the head that I shall bruise. It's a great deception. Do you see it? See how this posture of the scribes and Pharisees attempts to alter My identity and purpose? Can you see, My precious disciples… I am He, the Christ, the Promised Seed? This twisting is something you will have to stand against and expose all your days. Now I tell you before it comes, that when it comes to pass, you may believe that I am He."

After Jesus said this, He became troubled in spirit and declared,

"Most assuredly, I say to you, one of you will betray Me" (John 13:21).

The disciples seemed to be a bit perplexed as to whom Jesus was speaking of, so He exposed the hand of Satan:

Jesus answered, "It is he to whom I shall give a piece of bread when I have dipped *it*." And having dipped the bread, He gave *it* to Judas Iscariot, *the son* of Simon. Now after the piece of bread, Satan entered him. Then Jesus said to him, "What you do, do quickly" (John 13:26-27).

Judas was no ordinary guy with a slight case of demonic oppression. Judas was a full-on Nephilim in league with Satan. This enabled Satan to easily enter into Judas to empower him.

In His High Priestly Prayer, Jesus identified Judas as the "son of perdition," relating him with his father the devil (John 17:12).

Judas gives us a glimpse of those who, of like mind and spirit, will comprise the false prophet, the antichrist, and the false bride of Satan.

Judas was the false bride of the Revelation 17 church of Satan. He could never be the Bride of Christ. As true of all his line, he found no place for repentance, so he went and hanged himself, releasing the host of wicked spirits in him to manifest at a later time.

This isn't the first, nor will it be the last time, a religious organization will become the womb of the serpent seed, of which Judas was a type and shadow.

When Jesus called Judas a devil, it was the same word used in the passages declaring how Jesus was led by the Spirit into the wilderness to be tempted by the devil. Can it be any clearer?

Those Who Repent Will Be Saved

I'm by no means suggesting every mean and/or unbelieving person is a Nephilim. There are scores of Scriptures that describe born-again saints as once being among those who practiced despicable sins. People have been saved out of the depths of unbelief, witchcraft, and Satanism. God's power to save can give life to the vilest sinner who confesses their sin, who believes and repents of their ways. "And that they may recover themselves out of the snare of the devil, who are taken captive by him at his will" (2 Timothy 2:26 KJV). Yet there are others among us that are not fully of this world; even if they believe, they have no place for redemption. Being bound in iniquity and bitterness, they have no desire or ability for repentance. They only want to avoid the judgment (Acts 8:9-24; 13:6-12).

Going back just for a moment to the discussion Jesus was having with a large gathering of disciples, listen to what Jesus says:

> And He said, "Therefore I have said to you that no one can come to Me unless it has been granted to him by My Father" (John 6:65).

This statement was so shocking, all but the Twelve turned away from Jesus.

Many have accessed and experienced supernatural power, even supernatural life apart from Christ. John 10 tells us these are thieves and robbers whose end is sure. These thieves have accessed supernatural power illegitimately from the wrong source in the wrong place. They have pulled from the fallen powers in the second heaven, rather in the third heaven that Paul describes as the paradise of God. Those who have come up the wrong way need to repent and come the right way. God will grant access to Christ to all who will come and acknowledge Him as Savior and Lord. To these, Jesus will allow access to the Father. To all others, access is denied:

> Jesus said to him, "I am the way, the truth, and the life. No one comes to the Father except through Me" (John 14:6).

The Judas to Come

Why did Jesus choose Judas?

- To show us we are to love our enemies?
- To show us an example that all those among us may not really be *with* us?
- To reveal the stealth ability of the enemy?
- To prepare us for deceptive acts in our time?

Yes, all these have validity, but the Scripture gives us the answer. Jesus chose Judas to expose the serpent seed's great twisting of Scripture that was and is to come through the voices of a religious system called Mystery Babylon – the world church of the antichrist, the antichrist who will one day declare himself to be God. This is the Nephilim Agenda, the agenda of the future man of perdition. A Judas to come.

CHAPTER 6

WHERE DO DEMONS COME FROM?

Right after I was born again, I became involved in deliverance ministry. After six weeks of discipleship, I had cast a demon out of a person. I continued in this ministry for the next several years, experiencing supernatural phenomenon and power. The things a demon could cause a person to do never ceased to amaze me: sin, sickness, disease, contortions, smells, and incredible power. The unseen world of darkness was at work everywhere.

Just when I thought I had seen and heard it all, I began making trips to Africa. I began to see and experience things you would only see on the Sci Fi Channel: shape shifters, werewolves, and mermaid-like water demons to name a few. I experienced spirit translations and demon-possessed people astral projecting themselves into my presence. Incubi and succubi spirits attempted to assault me while I was asleep. I could go on, but I think you get the point.

Not a teacher, but rather the Lord Himself, finally taught me how to protect my family and myself from unwelcome intruders. I thought this kind of activity was normal for Christians at first.

It wasn't long before I discovered most Christians have never cast out a demon; even worse, many don't believe they exist. If they do exist, they can't bother them. After I cast demon after demon off and/or out of Christians, I was convinced there must be a terrible misunderstanding in Christian circles about what demons are, what they can do, and where they are from.

My good friend, Georgian Banov, tells me that over 80 percent of Bible commentaries are written by conservative scholars who have little or no experience in things of the Spirit beyond salvation. If this is the case, it would explain why so many Christians are oppressed, scared, or uneducated about the very real world of demonic activity. I believe it will be of utmost importance for all believers in the days ahead to be able to effectively identify demonic activity and deal with it victoriously!

What Are Demons?

Many conservative scholars suggest demons are fallen angels, specifically those who fell with Satan in the rebellion. They conclude this primarily from their understanding that angels are spirits (Ezekiel 28:14-16; Revelation 12:4).

Others hold that a pre-Adamic race existed between Genesis 1:1 and 1:2. They believe, before Adam, the earth was populated with cities and citizens. Lucifer was God's ruler. Through pride and rebellion Lucifer fell, taking one-third of the angels with him (Isaiah 45:18; Jeremiah 4:23-26; Isaiah 14:12-17; Revelation 12:5). This view concludes demons are the disembodied spirits of fallen angels.

The other predominate view postulates demons are the disembodied spirits of the offspring of the fallen watcher angels destroyed in the flood and subsequent judgments of God.

This last view best describes my understanding and experience in practical deliverance, scriptural study, and historical documents. While a pre-Adamic race is plausible, it isn't essential for demons to be disembodied spirits. What is clear is that the Bible is written for the Adamic race and the Gospel is for the salvation of man, not for angels or demons or hybrids. It seems clear to me that demons are the disembodied spirits of the union between the daughters of men and the sons of God. These unions took place before and after the flood according to Genesis 6:4.

THE DIFFERENCE BETWEEN DEMONS AND FALLEN ANGELS

The fallen angels who were not chained in Tartarus, who presently inhabit heavenly places (Ephesians 6:12; Matthew 12:24-25; Mark 5:2-9), are very powerful. They freely come and go between heaven and earth. Their goal is to be as human like in appearance as possible.

Fallen angels have their own bodies and therefore have no need to inhabit one. These fallen angels can shape shift into human form for extended periods of time, becoming like the holy angels who visited Abraham, and then Lot in Sodom and Gomorrah, and others in Scripture.

Watching the terminology of Jesus and the apostle Paul, they describe fallen angels, including Satan, as "devils" or "wicked spirits." Demons are called "unclean spirits" being the offspring of angels and humans. They are also simply called demons.

Demons seek out bodies to inhabit. If they are cast out of their hosts, they will go into animals to avoid roaming in desolate places (Mark 5:12-13; Luke 11:24-26; 1 Peter 5:8). If the demon finds no new host, he will seek to return to the one he has been cast out of with seven more spirits more wicked than himself.

Jesus commanded us to cast out demons. He gave us authority to bind, loose, and plunder the various classes of fallen angels through prayer and proclamation. We are able to battle and overcome all classes of fallen angels and demons, being complete in Christ Jesus. He is the head of all principality and power (Matthew 10:8; Colossians 2:9-10).

Angels can fly and move through the spirit realm in heavenly places. Demons are earth bound and must walk (Matthew 12:43).

THE SPIRITUAL MAKEUP OF NEPHILIM

The Bible isn't clear as to the spiritual makeup of the Nephilim in physical form or their disembodied state. We do know from the Genesis account that a seed, if unaltered, reproduces after its own kind. Therefore, an altered seed would be a hybrid containing similarities of both influences. The Hebrew language makes it clear that once air enters the lungs, life functions begin, and man or its similitude becomes a living soul. So one could conclude there is a semblance of a soul in the Nephilim. The offspring's spirit would come from the nature of the parents and ultimately from God who is the Father of spirits (Hebrews 12:9).

The exception is the case of the Nephilim and subsequent generations of their offspring. It is clear that angels are spirits and demons are unclean spirits. Therefore, a demon's spirit is a corruption of God's original design. The light that is in them is darkness and their soul is empty, void of humanity. It operates instinctively, like an animal, according to all accounts. Nephilim in body or demons out of body are God haters. They fear and despise Christ Jesus and those conformed into His likeness by new birth. Male or female, they are seductive, destructive, and killers of humanity (John 10:10).

Spirits are immortal. The Bible is clear: Jesus died in the flesh and was raised in the spirit as a spirit man. So shall those be who are His (1 Corinthians 15:35-49). It is the Holy Spirit who gives life to the mortal body and the Holy Spirit did not give life to the Nephilim, nor will He ever do so (Romans 8:9-11). Therefore, the eternal Nephilim spirit awaits only judgment and destruction.

Different Classes of Fallen Angels and Demons

The apostle Paul and Jesus also describe their different classes and dwelling places:

> For we wrestle not against flesh and blood, but against principalities, against powers, against the rulers of the darkness of this world, against spiritual wickedness in high places (Ephesians 6:12 KJV).

Demons are the manifested power of wickedness in the world. A hierarchy of fallen angels are the directing spiritual forces in heavenly places (see Ephesians 6:12).

When Jesus was teaching His disciples how to pray, He told them as they would ask, seek and knock that they could have confidence:

> "So I say to you, ask, and it will be given to you; seek, and you will find; knock, and it will be opened to you. For everyone who asks receives, and he who seeks finds, and to him who knocks it will be opened. If a son asks for bread from any father among you, will he give him a stone? Or if *he asks* for a fish, will he give him a serpent instead of a fish? Or if he asks for an egg, will he offer him a scorpion? If you then, being evil, know how to give good gifts to your children, how much more will *your* heavenly Father give the Holy Spirit to those who ask Him!" (Luke 11:9-13)

Jesus began to compare God the Father to earthly fathers. If you look at the text closely, it suggests that if a son asked for something, his father could direct him to an idol. The petitioning of this idol could produce what was desired. The demonically charged idols of stone, or the entity of a serpent or scorpion could produce other things. Jesus assured them God the Father would give His sons the Holy Spirit who would lead them to all they needed in Christ Jesus. God would not attach them to idols or wicked spirits. With this understanding they could ask for the Holy Spirit and be assured they would not receive something else.

If you look just a bit deeper, Jesus seems to be indicating, like Paul did, two different classes of evil beings: snake and scorpions.

These are the very beings described in the gospel of Luke as "all the power of the enemy." The snakes are the spiritual hosts of wickedness in heavenly places; the scorpions are the principalities and powers and rulers of darkness, those in the earth who take on flesh and blood. Jesus has conquered all of these and put them under our feet (see Luke 10:19).

The angels that were cast out of heaven seem to be different than those who willingly left their first estate (Jude 6). There is a big difference between abandoning one's home and being kicked out of the house. The book of Jubilees tells us that the watcher angels that first came to earth came to instruct humanity in righteousness and justice.

It is these watchers who first left their own estate to permanently take on human form and remain on earth. These are the ones Peter tells us are locked away in prison, so their form and their spirit is chained. Therefore, it is the disembodied spirits of the Nephilim who are the demons that asked Jesus, "Have you come here to torture us before the appointed time?" (Matthew

8:29 NIV). These are demons ruled over by Satan and the fallen, unchained, rebel angels.

Demon Spirits

These evil, demon spirits are identified by Enoch:

And now, the giants, who are produced from the spirits and flesh, shall be called evil spirits upon the earth, and on the earth shall be their dwelling. Evil spirits have proceeded from their bodies; because they are born from men, and from the holy Watchers is their beginning and primal origin; they shall be evil spirits on earth, and evil spirits shall they be called. (As for the spirits of heaven, in heaven shall be their dwelling, but as for the spirits of the earth which were born upon the earth, on the earth shall be their dwelling.) And the spirits of the giants afflict, oppress, destroy, attack, do battle, and work destruction on the earth, and cause trouble: they take no food, but nevertheless hunger and thirst, and cause offences. And these spirits shall rise up against the children of men and against the women, because they have proceeded from them (Enoch 15:8-12).[14]

Demons are on earth and never seen in heavenly places (Matthew 12:4; Mark 5:1-3). Jesus has given us all authority in the earth to make disciples and set captives free (Matthew 28:18-20). He has given us armor to protect us, and authority to pray and proclaim God's Word to battle and overcome the fallen angels in the second heaven. As we release the Word of God into our environment and atmosphere, the holy angels of God are active on our behalf to battle in the unseen realm (see Psalm 103:20).

---

[14] Charles, R. H. *The Book of Enoch* 15:8-12, pg 36-37. Escondido, California: The Book Tree © 1999.

It is very important to remind ourselves that God is a good God; He did not create evil spirits or the Nephilim. He is not responsible for evil, sin, sickness, disease, or destruction. He created Lucifer as a beautiful, pure cherub. It was Lucifer who gave in to pride and led rebellion against God. Lucifer took on the title of Satan – the enemy of God.

Devils and demons must submit to the name and person of Christ Jesus who lives in all born-again believers (Mark 1:34; Luke 4:40-41).

This book is not intended to provide a full theology on demons and devils, rather to reveal an aspect of what has been and what will increasingly be their mode of operation. Having said that, I have listed below a brief view of how demons operate in our lives and our world. In the appendix, I have also listed the sixteen strongmen unmasked in Scripture, to provide more understanding of their activities. This list will be beneficial for ministry and deliverance.

Characteristics of Demons

- Demons prefer to inhabit bodies rather than existing in a disembodied state.
  (Matthew 12:43-44; Revelation 18:2).

- Demons often live and operate together.
  (Mark 5:9; 16:9)

- Demons have a will and intellect, and varying levels of wickedness, endurance, and power.
  (Matthew 17:21; Mark 5:6-13)

WHERE DO DEMONS COME FROM?

- Demons have certain traits and personalities. They are intelligent; they seek to exercise their will.
  (Matthew 9:20-32; Luke 4:33-35; James 2:19)

- Demons in their disembodied form are mostly invisible to the natural eye.
  (Matthew 8:16; Luke 9:38-42)

- Demons can speak. They have feelings, emotions and desires.
  (Luke 4:41; Acts 8:7)

- Demons have names. Scripture refers to them as deaf spirits, deaf and dumb spirits, spirit of infirmity, etc.
  (Mark 9:25; Matthew 12:22; Luke 13:11)

- Demons know who Jesus is; they know their future and that believers have authority over them.
  (Luke 4:34, 41; Matthew 8:29; Acts 16:16-18; Luke 10:17-19)

- Demons dwell on earth until their future Judgment.
  (Matthew 12:43-45; 8:9)

CAPABILITY OF DEMONS

- Demons will fight against surrendering their host home.
  (Matthew 12:44; Luke 8:27-32; Mark 1:26)

- Demons are the primary source of sickness, disease, and oppression.
  (Acts 10:38)

- Demons exploit the flesh, providing sources of temptation and enticement to sin.
  (James 1:13-15; John 8:34)

- Demons wage war against the mind with fear, torment, oppression, and depression. They can cause emotional and mental breakdown, insanity, and suicide.
  (2 Timothy 1:7; Isaiah 61:3; Mark 5:15-16)

- Demons promote false doctrine, false prophetic utterance, and religion.
  (1 Timothy 4:1-2; 2 Corinthians 4:4; 11:3-4)

- Demons enslave people through addictive unclean habits such as alcoholism, drug abuse, sexual immorality, and perversion. Pornography is demonic in every aspect.
  (John 8:34; Romans 6:16)

- Demons can influence human events.
  (Revelation 16:13-14)

- Demons can speak through a person's voice and see through their eyes.
  (Mark 5:1-20; Acts 19:15)

- Demons can affect the state of their host person from total possession, to periodic oppression, to evil influence.
  (Matthew 12:43-45; Mark 5:2-8; 9:17-18)

Why do demons access humans?

- To fulfill Satan's desire to kill, steal, and destroy the Promised Seed and all who are made in the image and likeness of God.

- Satan wants the masses to acknowledge him as God, to worship him as God.
  (Isaiah 14:12-14; Luke 4:5-7)

- Bodies provide rest and shelter for demons and a means to manifest their evil desires.
  (Luke 11:24-26; 2 Timothy 2:25-26)

How do demons access humans?

- Sin provides demons with a foothold and legal right to enter.
  (1 Samuel 15:22; Luke 22:3-6; 1 Timothy 3:1-7; 6:9-10; Acts 5:2)

- Generational curses give place to familiar spirits that follow a bloodline for generations.
  (Exodus 34:7)

- Trauma. When we are unable to guard our hearts from which flow the issues of life – when faith is replaced with fear – our shields come down.
  (Proverbs 4:23; Hebrews 2:14-15)

- Broken covenant and coverings.
  (1 Corinthians 5:5; 1 Timothy 1:19,20)

- Doctrine of demons and rejecting truth.
  (2 Thessalonians 2:10-12)

This brief overview leaves no doubt about the destructive intent of demons and their role in the days ahead. These Nephilim spirits are unredeemable. The fallen angels, Satan, and the Nephilim demons will be judged by Christ after their defeat at the battle of Armageddon, as Christ returns to defeat Satan's plan to conquer the earth. They will be judged at the Great Throne Judgment after the Millennium and sentenced for eternity to the place prepared for them (Matthew 25:41).

And the angels who did not keep their proper domain, but left their own abode, He has reserved in everlasting chains under darkness for the judgment of the great day... Now Enoch, the seventh from Adam, prophesied about these men also, saying, "Behold, the Lord comes with ten thousands of His saints" (Jude 1:6, 14).

Until then, remember you have authority and power over all the power of the enemy. Let the freedom fighters arise!

CHAPTER 7

THE MYSTERY OF INIQUITY

The apostle Paul tells us the "mystery of iniquity" is already at work (2 Thessalonians 2:7 KJV). Daniel tells us that in the latter times, the operation of this mystery will come to fullness when the beast rises from the bottomless pit and unleashes all restraint (Daniel 8:23). It is of utmost importance this mystery of iniquity has no place or part in our lives now or in the days to come. Therefore, a clear understanding of the operation of iniquity is in order.

Deep within the heart of unredeemed man is a secret and often unspoken desire to satisfy the desires of the soul through the senses of the flesh. To satisfy the flesh, one believes they must trespass the boundaries of God – a belief that God, in some measure, is withholding something wonderful from us. Acting upon this premise, we commit lawlessness.

THE DEFINITION OF INIQUITY

Lawlessness is a good first definition of the operation of iniquity. In essence, we have declared God is not sufficient or willing to supply all our needs, so we go around Him.

This is the manner in which iniquity is activated and idolatry is perpetuated.

The Hebrew word for iniquity is *avon*, which means "perversity" and "depravity" in the sense of committing a crime.

God declares this depravity is done by those who hate Him. This seems shocking considering these words were given to a freshly delivered Hebrew nation: "I *am* the Lord your God, who brought you out of the land of Egypt, out of the house of bondage. You shall have no other gods before Me. You shall not make for yourself a carved image—any likeness *of anything* that *is* in heaven above, or that *is* in the earth beneath, or that *is* in the water under the earth; you shall not bow down to them nor serve them. For I, the Lord your God, *am* a jealous God, visiting the iniquity of the fathers upon the children to the third and fourth *generations* of those who hate Me" (Exodus 20:2-5).

The greater issue is that an iniquity doesn't stop with just one person, nor does it reoccur at the entry level over again. Iniquities are passed through the originator to the third or fourth generation in their bloodline. Worse yet, they are an open door for demonic exploitation that can spin them out of control.

Another definition of *avon* (ah-vone, Strong's #5771) is "weakness or tendency to fall under temptation." Iniquities operate by bringing thoughts, desires, and emotions we know are wrongful to a place of a least resistance. In this place, our desires are exploited by wicked and unclean spirits until we give in. To the extent the devil can control us through our secret desires to a place of sin is the degree he owns us and turns us from God. James describes the process like this:

> Let no one say when he is tempted, "I am tempted by God"; for God cannot be tempted by evil, nor does He Himself

tempt anyone. But each one is tempted when he is drawn away by his own desires and enticed. Then, when desire has conceived, it gives birth to sin; and sin, when it is full-grown, brings forth death. Do not be deceived, my beloved brethren. Every good gift and every perfect gift is from above, and comes down from the Father of lights, with whom there is no variation or shadow of turning (James 1:13-17).

It is important to note that temptation is not a sin. Jesus Himself was tempted, yet without sin. Lingering too long on a temptation is what gets us in trouble, and it is how we can become enticed by our own desires. A picture to help us understand how sin conceives is the "conception" that results from a completed sex act. The desire or temptation for sex is not sinful and does not produce conception. Conception only occurs when the desire is consummated into an act. Once desire is conceived (like a completed sex act), it's gone too far; sin has occurred and with each sin comes a measure of death. (Note that by no means is sex within marriage being condemned here. This is just an example to help explain the difference between temptation and sin.)

Iniquity works generationally; it builds generation after generation until it consumes you.

"But in the fourth generation they shall return here, for the iniquity of the Amorites *is* not yet complete" (Genesis 15:16).

When the morning dawned, the angels urged Lot to hurry, saying, "Arise, take your wife and your two daughters who are here, lest you be consumed in the punishment of the city" (Genesis 19:15).

The New Testament uses two different words to describe iniquity: Strong's #93, *adikia*, and Strong's #458, *anomia*. *Adikia* means a morally wrongful lifestyle in the implication of being wrongfully acquired. *Anomia* means illegality, violation, wickedness and lawlessness. A working definition of iniquity would be something like this: a wicked bent predisposing one to lawlessness to fulfill the desire of the flesh.

Iniquities are unique to each person and bloodline. What may be a sinful bent for some is not even a desire in others.

James asks us a very important question:

Where do wars and fights *come* from among you? Do *they* not *come* from your *desires for* pleasure that war in your members? You lust and do not have. You murder and covet and cannot obtain. You fight and war. Yet you do not have because you do not ask. You ask and do not receive, because you ask amiss, that you may spend *it* on your pleasures (James 4:1-3).

Where do the wars come from? James says, "The desires for pleasure that war in your members." Your members are the basic drives God has placed in each of us. These drives are meant to bring satisfaction to our lives and to bond us to God as we seek fulfillment according to His will.

The Six Basic Human Drives

There are six basic drives God has given to each of us. They are:
- Hunger
- Thirst
- Breathing

These are essentials for life. To these add:
- Gain of possessions
- Sexual drive
- Spiritual intuition

THE MYSTERY OF INIQUITY

All these drives function in us without us thinking of them. These drives are ever present and active in our everyday life. These are first seen activated by God's creation covenant over Adam and Eve:

> So God created man in His *own* image; in the image of God He created him; male and female He created them. Then God blessed them, and God said to them, "Be fruitful and multiply; fill the earth and subdue it; have dominion over the fish of the sea, over the birds of the air, and over every living thing that moves on the earth" (Genesis 1:27-28).

These six virtues are part of every healthy human. They are in our DNA code. The Lord desires that we look to Him for direction, instruction, and fulfillment of these drives in a manner that is consistent with His Kingdom.

Satan Uses Our Drives Against Us

Satan, knowing these drives are present, seeks to exploit them through counterfeit means, evoking lawlessness. Once the hook is set, the mystery of iniquity, that hidden principle of rebellion against authority, is in full motion. Now Satan has a measure of ownership and control over us and he can manifest his wickedness. For example:

Food and drink

Our intrinsic drive for food and drink becomes corrupted. Excessiveness kicks in, leading to gluttony, alcoholism, or some excessive, uncontrollable appetite.

Possessions

Regarding gain of possessions, most all of us, if we are truthful, would be delighted with something bigger, better, newer, more expensive or expansive.

The drive isn't wrong, but the way we go about fulfilling it can get us into trouble. King David puts it this way:

> O Lord, *You are* the portion of my inheritance and my cup; You maintain my lot. The lines have fallen to me in pleasant *places*; Yes, I have a good inheritance. I will bless the Lord who has given me counsel; My heart also instructs me in the night seasons. I have set the Lord always before me; Because *He is* at my right hand I shall not be moved (Psalm 16:5-8).

In other words, with thanksgiving, we enjoy the blessings of the Lord. It is okay to desire and acquire more things as long as you own them and they don't own you.

The apostle Paul learned to be content in a variety of situations, because he understood he was in the will of God. The devil exploits this drive with the spirit of greed, covetousness, and pride.

SEXUALITY

Our sexual drive has historically been Satan's most effective area. He has moved through the spirit of Baal with sexual exploitation, pornography, and perversion. God desires our sexual drive to be fulfilled in the context of marriage. The intimacy between a husband and wife is wholesome and fulfilling. Children are often the fruit the Lord gives us.

SPIRITUAL INTUITION

Spiritual intuition is that inner drive, or the inner knowing that we are connected to a spiritual force greater than ourselves. This force is life giving and supernatural. This force is the living God, our heavenly Father. Nothing is more powerful or fulfilling than the affirming love of a father that he gives to his child.

Satan comes with a counterfeit offering, a partial truth that takes a multitude of religious forms. It is a form of godliness, but denies the power and relationship God freely extends through Christ Jesus.

How Strongholds Are Established

It is through one or more of these drives that evil wickedness seeks to find its way into the soul of man. Once a foothold is established, every subsequent generation will deal with their daddy's demons.

Identifying the operation of iniquities can be as easy as looking at what one struggles with in their own life. A look backwards through the family tree will confirm your struggle and highlight other issues as well. For example, child abuse, divorce, and alcoholism are often generational. Cancer and heart disease are generational diseases. Sometimes an iniquity will manifest differently because of the environment. The alcoholic tendencies of the father may hit the son, but because the son is raised in a religious environment intolerant of alcohol, the iniquity could manifest as a different uncontrollable appetite such as overeating.

Freedom From Nephilim Corruption

In the following pages, I have included a section from a deliverance manual I have published entitled, *Pulling Down Strongholds*, that helps one to deal with these iniquities. After reading about Nephilim, demons, and devils, you might wonder if you have had a brush with them. It is probable you have had a brush with these unclean and wicked spirits by the power of influence, doctrine of demons, temptation, and numerous other means. They bring lawlessness to every sector of human existence.

However, these encounters do not disqualify one from salvation and redemption. The true test you are a follower of Jesus Christ (and not Nephilim offspring) is the presence and witness of the Holy Spirit within yourself. Even if you have been fully demon-possessed, your spirit can be free and your soul made whole by the shed blood of Jesus Christ. The Holy Spirit loves to bear witness that you are in Christ Jesus as a result of your confession of faith in Him as Savior and acknowledgment of His Lordship over your life (see Romans 8:16).

The apostle John also writes:

> If we receive the witness of men, the witness of God is greater; for this is the witness of God which He has testified of His Son. He who believes in the Son of God has the witness in himself (1 John 5:9-10).

God wants you to know you have been accepted, forgiven, and washed by the blood of Jesus Christ. Therefore, God sent the Holy Spirit into our hearts to give us assurance of life and salvation. Christ's body and blood will release us from every cord or stain of wickedness.

For those who are Nephilim biological offspring, they only want salvation from the coming judgment. However, just as it was in Noah's day, so it will be for them. They may have life by virtue of breath and a brain. But they lack the fullness of a soul and the fully human spirit they so desire. The only eternity that awaits them is the lake of fire. They have sworn allegiance to Lucifer and are not willing or able to change.

I encourage you to follow the prayer and instructions listed below to ensure your freedom from any Nephilim corruption.

Pulling Down Strongholds[15]

Satan may have gained access to your family by generational sins. If you have not taken up your identity and heritage in Christ, your passive posture to Satan is the same as your consent to bring familiar spirits and sinful tendencies to your bloodline. Many things predispose a person to certain behaviors (such as learned behavior or works of the flesh), but a look back into your family tree will often identify patterns of sin and unrighteousness, torment, and disease. You are not guilty of other's sin, but by acknowledging and renouncing it, you shut the door and remove the curse from you and your offspring. Jesus has broken every curse off you, but you must declare and receive your freedom. (These are specific generational patterns of sin, not necessarily any or all sin you have read about so far in this manual.)

Read Isaiah 53:1-5; Galatians 3:10-13; Matthew 8:16-17.

Grief: Spiritual and physical malady, anxiety, disease, sickness.

Sorrow: Spiritual and physical suffering, pain, grief, affliction, anguish.

Transgression: Our sin under the law, all sin before being born again (1 Peter 2:24-25; Galatians 3:10).

Iniquities: Sin, wickedness, evil bent, generational patterns of sin.

Pray: "Dear Heavenly Father, I understand that the sinful tendencies in my parents and forefathers that have not been dealt with by confession and repentance can be passed to me. They have opened a doorway for demonic oppression and activity in my life and generation. I understand that Christ's body was bruised for my iniquities and that He became a curse for me. Therefore, I ask You

---

[15] From *Pulling Down Strongholds*, pgs 24-25

to reveal to me any generational iniquities that have been passed to me so I can be free. I choose to honor my mother and father and glorify the Lord Jesus in my body. In Jesus' Name, Amen."

In dealing with generational iniquities, it is necessary at times to identify the "strongman" and deal with the particular manifestations under that strongman through renunciation and prayer. See Addendum A for a list of 16 strongmen that have biblical references.

Common Iniquities to Consider:

Greed   Lust   Abuse   Alcoholism   Drug Use   Pride
Anger   Adultery   Covenant breaking   False Religions

Other iniquities you see in your life or in your family line

_____
_____
_____
_____

List all known generational patterns of sins and sicknesses:

_____
_____
_____

Iniquities (generational patterns of sin) are broken and removed by virtue of the bruised body of Christ, just as by faith our sins are removed and forgiven by the shed blood of Jesus. Even so, our iniquities are removed by faith in the bruised body of Christ. By faith we place our sins "under the blood." By faith we place our iniquities "upon the body" of Christ. Picture in your mind's eye your iniquity removed from you and placed upon Jesus' body on the cross. By faith, their position and power in your life are removed and broken.

Pray: "Dear Lord, just as Nehemiah, Daniel, Jeremiah and others acknowledged their sins, the iniquity of their forefathers and their nation, even so I acknowledge the idolatry, sins, and iniquity of my forefathers and our nation. As Your people we have turned aside from You, the only true and living God (Isaiah 53:6; Nehemiah 1:5-11; Daniel 9:1-19).

I confess our rebellion and sinfulness. I ask You to cleanse and purify my family and myself, releasing us from strongholds over our lives. By faith, I place my iniquities and sin including _____ upon the body of Christ and under His shed blood. I thank You for releasing me from the operation of these iniquities in my life by becoming a curse for me. I thank You that by Your stripes I am healed."

By dealing with generational iniquities, you have become free from Nephilim contamination that may have influenced your bloodline at some point. Consider these parting exhortations:

> And having been set free from sin, you became slaves of righteousness. I speak in human *terms* because of the weakness of your flesh. For just as you presented your members *as* slaves of uncleanness, and of lawlessness *leading* to *more* lawlessness, so now present your members *as* slaves *of* righteousness for holiness (Romans 6:18-19).

> For the grace of God that brings salvation has appeared to all men, teaching us that, denying ungodliness and worldly lusts, we should live soberly, righteously, and godly in the present age, looking for the blessed hope and glorious appearing of our great God and Savior Jesus Christ, who gave

Himself for us, that He might redeem us from every lawless deed and purify for Himself *His* own special people, zealous for good works (Titus 2:11-14).

Once you are free from the overpowering force of iniquities doesn't mean you won't be tempted again. However, this time the temptation and desire can easily be denied. Understanding this will help prepare you for the days to come and encourage you to be an overcomer in Christ as He desires.

Iniquity Prepares the Way

The mystery of iniquity will continue to operate in the souls of unredeemed man through a new operation of Nephilim already at work. They will make a way for the false prophet, the antichrist/beast and Satan himself through a deceptive one-world religion.

Mystery Babylon is the compilation of the working of the mystery of iniquity. We must rid ourselves of the operation of iniquities in our midst because the days of Noah are returning for a second curtain call.

CHAPTER 8

AS IT WAS IN THE DAYS OF NOAH

In a sincere and probing encounter, the disciples came to Jesus privately, saying, "Tell us, when will these things be? And what will be the sign of Your coming, and of the end of the age?" (Matthew 24:3)

This engaging question was put before Jesus just after He had announced the destruction of the temple and the end of things as they knew them. Jesus begins a lengthy reply outlining several events and conditions that would precede His return. About midstream into the conversation He brings forth an insightful view of the past to help us understand our future.

> "But of that day and hour no one knows, not even the angels of heaven, but My Father only. But as the days of Noah *were*, so also will the coming of the Son of Man be. For as in the days before the flood, they were eating and drinking, marrying and giving in marriage, until the day that Noah entered the ark, and did not know until the flood came and took them all away, so also will the coming of the Son of Man be" (Matthew 24:36-39).

Nothing seems out of the ordinary here at first glance. At worst, just a bunch of clueless people plunging headlong toward disaster while living normal lives. The wars, earthquakes, and other world upheaval has become commonplace. To stop at this conclusion would render one as unprepared for what's coming as those we suppose to be clueless.

The Days of Noah Will Repeat Themselves

Jesus clearly said, "As it was in the days of Noah." Think back through the pages you have read regarding the conditions, the activities, and events in Noah's time that led to the destruction of the known world by a flood. Now you are getting a sense of reality of what was and what is to come. Lest we become like the frog in the proverbial kettle, listen to what the apostle Paul wrote to Timothy concerning the last days:

> But know this, that in the last days perilous times will come: For men will be lovers of themselves, lovers of money, boasters, proud, blasphemers, disobedient to parents, unthankful, unholy, unloving, unforgiving, slanderers, without self-control, brutal, despisers of good, traitors, headstrong, haughty, lovers of pleasure rather than lovers of God, having a form of godliness but denying its power. And from such people turn away! For of this sort are those who creep into households and make captives of gullible women loaded down with sins, led away by various lusts, always learning and never able to come to the knowledge of the truth. Now as Jannes and Jambres resisted Moses, so do these also resist the truth: men of corrupt minds, disapproved concerning the faith; but they will progress no further, for their folly will be manifest to all, as theirs also was (2 Timothy 3:1-9).

You might say, "The world is already like this." Yes, it is, but it hasn't yet reached the level of the days of Noah. We have experienced DNA manipulation of crops and animals again, but no dinosaur sized creatures yet. In the days of Noah, giant Nephilim were openly living among the people. Fallen angels posing as demigods would manifest in the earth to be worshipped. They would take for themselves wives of their choosing. Drunken orgies and feasting of these giants began to consume animal and man. Every sort of evil and perversion was on the earth while Noah was living and preaching righteousness.

If you have the stomach for it, follow along these next few pages to see how the days of Noah will repeat themselves resulting once again in the destruction of evil off the earth.

Fallen Angels, the Nephilim, and Open Wickedness

The Gospel of Luke provides for us another account of Jesus answering questions about the end of the age and the coming of the Kingdom.

This time, it's the Pharisees asking the questions instead of the disciples, but Jesus uses the occasion to reinforce what He wanted the disciples to understand.

> And as it was in the days of Noah, so it will be also in the days of the Son of Man: They ate, they drank, they married wives, they were given in marriage, until the day that Noah entered the ark, and the flood came and destroyed them all (Luke 17:26-27).

I want to draw your attention to the word, "They." Nothing is unusual about people eating, drinking, or being given in marriage. Foregoing the obvious, remember the Genesis account:

The sons of God saw the daughters of men, that they *were* beautiful; and they took wives for themselves of all whom they chose. And the Lord said, "My Spirit shall not strive with man forever, for he *is* indeed flesh; yet his days shall be one hundred and twenty years." There were giants on the earth in those days, and also afterward, when the sons of God came in to the daughters of men and they bore *children* to them. Those *were* the mighty men who *were* of old, men of renown (**Genesis 6:2-4**).

Jesus is telling us the "they" included not just men and women, but also fallen angels and the giant Nephilim. And if that's not strong enough, Jesus then puts the activities of Sodom into the answer to leave no doubt in our minds of the open wickedness that shall come upon the earth. Likewise, as it was also in the days of Lot: They ate, they drank, they bought, they sold, they planted, they built; but on the day that Lot went out of Sodom it rained fire and brimstone from heaven and destroyed *them* all (Luke 17:28-29).

For now, this activity is being somewhat restrained, yet ramping up to maturity as the wheat and the tares come up together.

False Worship of Evil Beings

The New Testament records an encounter with a priest of Zeus (Acts 14:8-18). In Lystra, a group of people was present who worshipped planetary entities and star gods. When they witnessed the power of God through Paul and Barnabas, they declared, "The gods have come down in the likeness of men." It is evident these people had experienced visitations of gods from other planets – in particular, the gods of Jupiter and Mars who exercised shape shifting abilities.

It is amazing how quickly they began to worship Paul and Barnabas as gods. Even so, we will see false worship of manifested evil beings that display supernatural power in the days ahead. These also will be a force of resistance against the preaching of the gospel (Acts 8:10; 12:22; 28:26).

BEASTS WHO FIGHT AGAINST THE GOSPEL

In 1 Corinthians, the apostle Paul says he fought with beasts, beasts that knew they would not rise again:

> I affirm, by the boasting in you which I have in Christ Jesus our Lord, I die daily. If, in the manner of men, I have fought with beasts at Ephesus, what advantage *is it* to me? If *the* dead do not rise, *"Let us eat and drink, for tomorrow we die!"* (1 Corinthians 15:31-32).

It appears Paul had resistance in preaching the gospel from the Nephilim, those who have no regard for God or life. Those, who, like in the days of Noah were eating and drinking, "for tomorrow we die." Peter echoes Paul's assessment in 2 Peter:

> By covetousness they will exploit you with deceptive words; for a long time their judgment has not been idle, and their destruction does not slumber.... But these, like natural brute beasts made to be caught and destroyed, speak evil of the things they do not understand, and will utterly perish in their own corruption, *and* will receive the wages of unrighteousness, *as* those who count it pleasure to carouse in the daytime. *They are* spots and blemishes, carousing in their own deceptions while they feast with you, having eyes full of adultery and that cannot cease from sin, enticing unstable souls. *They have* a heart trained in covetous practices, *and are* accursed children (2 Peter 2:3, 12-14).

False Prophets and False Teachers

The serpent seed will be in the ranks of secular society as well as in the arena of religion. Peter tells us there will be false prophets and false teachers among the people, who will secretly bring in destructive heresies, even denying the Lord. The way of truth will be blasphemed, resulting in their doom and destruction.

> These are wells without water, clouds carried by a tempest, for whom is reserved the blackness of darkness forever. For when they speak great swelling *words* of emptiness, they allure through the lusts of the flesh, through lewdness, the ones who have actually escaped from those who live in error (2 Peter 2:17-18).

Nephilim Offspring Openly Among Us

The manifestation of the Nephilim will begin to increase in the days ahead as the fourth Kingdom arises and comes into maturity. The Nephilim that once lived openly among us will attempt with a measure of success to do so again. Daniel describes this fourth Kingdom from Nebuchadnezzar's dream:

> And the fourth kingdom shall be as strong as iron, inasmuch as iron breaks in pieces and shatters everything; and like iron that crushes, *that kingdom* will break in pieces and crush all the others. Whereas you saw the feet and toes, partly of potter's clay and partly of iron, the kingdom shall be divided; yet the strength of the iron shall be in it, just as you saw the iron mixed with ceramic clay. And *as* the toes of the feet *were* partly of iron and partly of clay, *so* the kingdom shall be partly strong and partly fragile (Daniel 2:40-42).

The feet of the giant are made partly of potter's clay and partly of iron. The understanding is this: Clay is representative of man, made of the dust of the earth, a vessel for the Holy Spirit. Iron is symbolic of rule. Jesus will rule with a rod of iron, so the antichrist's counterfeit kingdom uses the same language. Iron has been used throughout biblical history to defeat Israel and resist the way of the gospel.

Thus, this end-time Satanic kingdom comes forth with deceptive form. It is the mixing of the iron and clay that is alarming and insightful. What happened in the days of Noah will happen again to produce a Nephilim offspring of civilians and soldiers set out to overthrow the Kingdom of God.

> As you saw iron mixed with ceramic clay, they will mingle with the seed of men; but they will not adhere to one another, just as iron does not mix with clay (Daniel 2:43).

Notice "they" will mingle with the seed of men. A new wave of fallen angels will seek out strange flesh again just as the Nephilim have continued to do throughout the generations. They are beings that will be half human, half celestial once again. These may not be giant in size or horrible in appearance due to years of possible DNA code alteration. But, then again, with what's coming, who would notice?

> Let no one deceive you by any means; for *that Day will not come* unless the falling away comes first, and the man of sin is revealed, the son of perdition, who opposes and exalts himself above all that is called God or that is worshiped, so that he sits as God in the temple of God, showing himself that he is God (2 Thessalonians 2:3-4).

TERROR AND DECEPTION

Prior to this event, the world will experience evil even greater than Noah's worst day. The restraints of evil will soon come off. It will unleash terror and deception beyond imaginations:

> And now you know what is restraining, that he may be revealed in his own time. For the mystery of lawlessness is already at work; only He who now restrains *will do so* until He is taken out of the way. And then the lawless one will be revealed, whom the Lord will consume with the breath of His mouth and destroy with the brightness of His coming (2 Thessalonians 2:6-8).

As God has always done in the past, so shall He do again. He will wait until wickedness and depravity reach its fullness, then He will come forth with judgment against evil and redemption for those who have made themselves Christ's.

THE FALLING AWAY

There is a future event coming that will fully embody the words, "shock and awe." What has happened in part though the ages will now progressively become a marked and measured event. It is the event that will go hand in hand at the revelation of the lawless one, the man of sin, the son of perdition.

Paul calls it the "falling away" (2 Thessalonians 2:3). He describes it in his letter to Timothy as a departure from the faith (1 Timothy 4:1-3). This isn't talking about a few people leaving church, rather a wave of deception so great that it can only be compared with the days of Noah, when even the godly line of Seth was seduced and only Noah remained untainted in his gene pool. In short succession, when He who restrains takes the restraint off, literally all hell will break loose for a period of time, specifically the last 42 months of the tribulation period (Revelation 13:5).

Let's consider the words of Paul a little more closely regarding the great apostasy, the falling away and the restraint that is currently in place:

> And now you know what is restraining, that he may be revealed in his own time (2 Thessalonians 2:6).

"What is restraining" is in the neutral form, indicating it's not a person, rather a place. The place is the infamous abyss where the fallen watchers angels among others are currently imprisoned (Revelation 9:1-10; 2 Peter 2:4). This place, the abyss, is restraining the antichrist/beast from being revealed at this time, so he may be revealed at the appointed time. Satan has always tried to change the times and law (Daniel 7:25). This will be high on the agenda of the antichrist as well. He will attempt to change feast and festival days, holy days, and the Sabbath. Satan wants the time changed now so he can bring forth his lying signs and wonders before the believing world is ready. The Bible is clear about who is in control of the times and seasons: Daniel answered and said: "Blessed be the name of God forever and ever, For wisdom and might are His. And He changes the times and the seasons; He removes kings and raises up kings; He gives wisdom to the wise And knowledge to those who have understanding" (Daniel 2:20-21).

Jesus, speaking to the disciples, also said that not even the angels in heaven knew, but that His Father alone determines the timing of events (Matthew 24:36; Acts 1:7).

With this understanding, the next verse can be understood:

> For the mystery of lawlessness is already at work; only He who now restrains *will do so* until He is taken out of the way (2 Thessalonians 2:7).

He who now restrains the full onslaught of evil upon the earth is He who is in control of the times and seasons. This lofty power is in the hands of God alone. He (God) restrains until he (the angel with the key to the bottomless pit) opens the pit and is taken out of the way. He (God) controls the moment that he who is not god, rather the beast – the king of the bottomless pit, is released. In the sweeping course of events at this time, the beast/antichrist will be released from the bottomless pit. When he is released, he will unleash much of the content of the abyss into the world.

The Antichrist

At this same point in mid-tribulations, Satan and his angels will be cast out of heaven to the earth with much wrath (Revelations 12:4). Satan, who will now be earthbound, will empower and possess the antichrist. He will become the manifested abomination of desolation who takes his place in the temple to be worshipped as God.

The antichrist/beast will work signs and wonders like Christ did at His coming to cause those who did not love the truth to fall away and begin to worship the beast. This event will draw much of the world from any form of attachment to God to allegiance to the antichrist as Paul said (2 Thessalonians 2:3).

The next 42 months will be unrestrained, unchecked evil of every sort as it was in the days of Noah. The antichrist will gather all the armies of earth to join with the Nephilim and the rest of the wicked angels for the war of all wars called Armageddon. Then Jude 14 and 15 will come to pass, the prophesy of Enoch, just after the fulfillment of Acts 2:18-21. Read again the book of Jude with your new found understanding:

Jude, a bondservant of Jesus Christ, and brother of James,
To those who are called, sanctified by God the Father,

and preserved in Jesus Christ: Mercy, peace, and love be multiplied to you.

Beloved, while I was very diligent to write to you concerning our common salvation, I found it necessary to write to you exhorting you to contend earnestly for the faith which was once for all delivered to the saints. For certain men have crept in unnoticed, who long ago were marked out for this condemnation, ungodly men, who turn the grace of our God into lewdness and deny the only Lord God and our Lord Jesus Christ.

But I want to remind you, though you once knew this, that the Lord, having saved the people out of the land of Egypt, afterward destroyed those who did not believe. And the angels who did not keep their proper domain, but left their own abode, He has reserved in everlasting chains under darkness for the judgment of the great day; as Sodom and Gomorrah, and the cities around them in a similar manner to these, having given themselves over to sexual immorality and gone after strange flesh, are set forth as an example, suffering the vengeance of eternal fire. Likewise also these dreamers defile the flesh, reject authority, and speak evil of dignitaries. Yet Michael the archangel, in contending with the devil, when he disputed about the body of Moses, dared not bring against him a reviling accusation, but said, "The Lord rebuke you!" But these speak evil of whatever they do not know; and whatever they know naturally, like brute beasts, in these things they corrupt themselves. Woe to them! For they have gone in the way of Cain, have run greedily in the error of Balaam for profit, and perished in the rebellion of Korah.

These are spots in your love feasts, while they feast with you without fear, serving *only* themselves. *They are* clouds without water, carried about by the winds; late autumn trees without fruit, twice dead, pulled up by the roots; raging waves of the sea, foaming up their own shame; wandering stars for whom is reserved the blackness of darkness forever. Now Enoch, the seventh from Adam, prophesied about these men also, saying, "Behold, the Lord comes with ten thousands of His saints, to execute judgment on all, to convict all who are ungodly among them of all their ungodly deeds which they have committed in an ungodly way, and of all the harsh things which ungodly sinners have spoken against Him."

These are grumblers, complainers, walking according to their own lusts; and they mouth great swelling *words*, flattering people to gain advantage. But you, beloved, remember the words which were spoken before by the apostles of our Lord Jesus Christ: how they told you that there would be mockers in the last time who would walk according to their own ungodly lusts. These are sensual persons, who cause divisions, not having the Spirit.

But you, beloved, building yourselves up on your most holy faith, praying in the Holy Spirit, keep yourselves in the love of God, looking for the mercy of our Lord Jesus Christ unto eternal life. And on some have compassion, making a distinction; but others save with fear, pulling *them* out of the fire, hating even the garment defiled by the flesh.

Now to Him who is able to keep you from stumbling, And to present *you* faultless Before the presence of His glory with exceeding joy, To God our Savior, Who alone is wise, *Be* glory and majesty, Dominion and power, Both now and forever. Amen.

Much more could be said and written about these last days, but I think you get the point.

Regarding the identity of the antichrist, consider this: the lawless one shall ascend out of the bottomless pit. He is a person who existed before Revelation was written (A.D. 96); "he was" in power once, but wasn't when the Revelation was given; "he is not," but he will come forth again to perdition:

> The beast that you saw was, and is not, and will ascend out of the bottomless pit and go to perdition. And those who dwell on the earth will marvel, whose names are not written in the Book of Life from the foundation of the world, when they see the beast that was, and is not, and yet is (Revelation 17:8).

This is the deceptive presentation of the antichrist beast that counterfeits the true Messiah, Christ Jesus. Jesus is the One who is and was and is to come (Revelation 1:4).

This king of the bottomless pit whose Hebrew name is Abaddon, in Greek, Apollyon, will come forth unrestrained after the first woe (Revelation 9:11). He will become the embodiment of Satan and empower the final stages of the Nephilim Agenda. These are those Christ will consume with the breath of His mouth and destroy with the brightness of His coming (2 Thessalonians 2:8).

ATTEMPT TO DESTROY ISRAEL

As if this isn't enough, the serpent seed of the line of Esau still has a score to settle with Jacob. Though Jacob and Esau reconciled to a degree, Jacob (the nation of Israel) has been looking over his shoulder ever since. The prophecy of his father Isaac is yet to be fulfilled:

Then Isaac his father answered and said to him: "Behold, your dwelling shall be of the fatness of the earth, And of the dew of heaven from above. By your sword you shall live, And you shall serve your brother; And it shall come to pass, when you become restless, That you shall break his yoke from your neck" (Genesis 27:39-40).

It is not a coincidence the last days are called the time of Jacob's trouble. Esau has become a servant to Jacob, but his bloodthirsty vengeance is yet to come. As the prophecy declares, the brothers will wrestle again:

"By your sword you shall live, And you shall serve your brother; And it shall come to pass, when you become restless, That you shall break his yoke from your neck" (Genesis 27:40).

In the last days, Esau will become restless and come after Jacob, comprised of the 12 tribes of Israel.

Esau, the serpent seed, will bring about a resurgence of Nephilim on the scene. These modern-day Nephilim have put on suits and ties. They are currently dwelling in the fatness of the earth and the dew of heaven. These Nephilim are in the upper levels of society in wealth and luxury. They are in aggressive and moderate religious systems. These places of opulent luxury have satisfied them for a time, but they are about to become restless and begin to move against Jacob. Those who are not in suits or holy garb are high-level military and police. These will be used by the antichrist to do his bidding:

He shall enter also into the glorious land, and many countries shall be overthrown: but these shall escape out of his hand, even Edom, and Moab, and the chief of the children of Ammon (Daniel 11:41 KJV).

Edom, Moab, and the prominent people of Ammon will escape the hand of the antichrist to pursue Esau's quest. These bad seeds will help gather the tribes of Israel to the sheepfold of Bozrah for annihilation. But they shall not prevail, for the Lord of the breakthrough will set them free:

"I will surely assemble all of you, O Jacob, I will surely gather the remnant of Israel; I will put them together like sheep of the fold, Like a flock in the midst of their pasture; They shall make a loud noise because of *so many* people. The one who breaks open will come up before them; They will break out, Pass through the gate, And go out by it; Their king will pass before them, With the Lord at their head" (Micah 2:12-13).

The Nephilim who seek to set the antichrist into place by terror and deception – the Nephilim who attempt to kill off the children of Israel – will all fail.

Who *is* this who comes from Edom, With dyed garments from Bozrah, This *One who is* glorious in His apparel, Traveling in the greatness of His strength?– "I who speak in righteousness, mighty to save. Why *is* Your apparel red, And Your garments like one who treads in the winepress?"

"I have trodden the winepress alone, And from the peoples no one *was* with Me. For I have trodden them in My anger, And trampled them in My fury; Their blood is sprinkled upon My garments, And I have stained all My robes. For the day of vengeance *is* in My heart, And the year of My redeemed has come" (Isaiah 63:1-4).

The Lord of the breakthrough shall come through right on time and bring great deliverance to His beloved people.

The Days of Noah Will Return to the Earth

The days of Noah shall return to the earth. Yet in the midst of these things, God is raising up His glorious Bride for His Son. In the midst of deep darkness, while all this is occurring, a bright light of hope shall arise – a glorious victorious bride. Multiple levels of deception are set to be released in our time to prepare the world to receive and worship the antichrist as God. Television and media have acquainted the masses with supernatural phenomenon and language. We are being conditioned to believe other worldly beings are friendly and false religions espousing the doctrine of demons are acceptable in society. In the days ahead, it will become critical to be able to discern the spirit behind the manifestation. John tells us we are to test the spirits (1 John 4:1), test the lifestyle, the fruit, and their confession (see Appendix B).

Every Spirit-filled believer should be able to discern the difference in operation between the human spirit, the Holy Spirit, and an evil spirit. Becoming a person of the Word of God is the best way to exercise oneself to discern both good and evil. Desiring the operation of the gift of discernment is of great value and should be fully sought often (1 Corinthians 12:10).

In these coming days of darkness, the prophet Isaiah tells us to, "Arise, shine; for your light has come! And the glory of the Lord is risen upon you" (Isaiah 60:1).

CHAPTER 9

THE BRIDE WITHOUT SPOT OR WRINKLE

Throughout Scripture, it is evident that God has taken great care to preserve the identity of the Promised Seed. It was important for people to be able to identify their heritage. Each generation lived hopeful lives, believing they may be the one from whom the promised Messiah would come. Every time a woman of the godly line became pregnant, she would wonder: *Am I the one who will birth the Savior?*

Men and women would keep themselves pure, overcoming the temptations of the day, waiting and preparing for the Messiah. This is much like us who are waiting once again for His coming. The difference is that this time, He is not coming as a baby ... a lamb to be slain.

This time He is coming as a lion, the Lion of the Tribe of Judah, to bring swift destruction upon the wicked and sweet redemption to the saints who are looking for His appearing. He is coming as the glorious Bridegroom for His Bride, the Seed of Abraham, who have been washed in His Blood, purified and made white. God is going to fulfill His covenant with His people through Christ Jesus, who is the ultimate fulfillment of the Seed of David.

GOD PRESERVES THE IDENTITY OF THE PROMISED SEED

It is no mistake that Cain is listed in the generations of the history of the heavens and earth. But then Seth is the first listed son in the line of Adam and Cain is excluded, being of the cursed serpent seed. As carefully as the Lord preserved the identity of the Promised Seed, even so, He has preserved the identity of the serpent seed.

When Abraham, Isaac, and the other fathers gave instruction to their sons regarding choosing a mate, they were explicit. They were not to take a wife for themselves from among the Canaanites. The Canaanites had become synonymous with the compilation of nations who embodied the serpent seed – the nations God commanded the Israelites to overcome and destroy (Genesis 24:3; 28:1).

Samson chose a pagan wife against the wishes of his parents, but never married her or produced children from her.

In the moving story of Hannah, she promised God she would dedicate her son to Him if He would take away the reproach of her barrenness. In her prayer of quiet weeping before God, Eli the priest observed her and was ready to dismiss her as just another corrupted woman. She was quick to seek his blessing, declaring she was not a daughter of Belial (1 Samuel 1:15-16). Through her God brought forth Samuel who brought correction and purity to the corrupted priesthood. God is still looking for those who will bring forth children – parents who will keep them in the ways of the Lord all their lives. God wants all born-again believers to exercise care in whom to marry. We are born again to overcome the curse in the earth:

> Since you have purified your souls in obeying the truth through the Spirit in sincere love of the brethren, love one another fervently with a pure heart, having been born again, not of corruptible seed but incorruptible, through the word of God which lives and abides forever (1 Peter 1:22-23).

In his second letter, Peter elaborates even more as to the ability and destiny we have in God through Christ Jesus:

> Grace and peace be multiplied to you in the knowledge of God and of Jesus our Lord, as His divine power has given to us all things that *pertain* to life and godliness, through the knowledge of Him who called us by glory and virtue, by which have been given to us exceedingly great and precious promises, that through these you may be partakers of the divine nature, having escaped the corruption *that is* in the world through lust (2 Peter 1:2-4).

WE MUST BE ALERT AND DISCERNING

As the Nephilim begin to resurface, they will target the Promised Seed in yet another attempt to pollute the gene pool. Once again they will seek to disqualify everyone possible. Fathers, you must be on alert and be the protective covering you are called to be:

> For if a woman is not covered, let her also be shorn. But if it is shameful for a woman to be shorn or shaved, let her be covered. For a man indeed ought not to cover *his* head, since he is the image and glory of God; but woman is the glory of man. For man is not from woman, but woman from man. Nor was man created for the woman, but woman for the man. For this reason the woman ought to have *a symbol of authority on her* head, because of the angels (1 Corinthians 11:6-10).

A new, more sophisticated Nephilim will come forth with wealth and desired expertise. Others will come with prowess and intrigue designed to draw one away into their agenda. History will repeat itself as Jesus said it would: They ate, they drank, they married wives, they were given in marriage (see Matthew 24:38). Paul exhorts us to no longer know a person just after the flesh, titles, positions, or orders; we are to know them after the spirit that is in them.

> Therefore, from now on, we regard no one according to the flesh. Even though we have known Christ according to the flesh, yet now we know *Him thus* no longer. Therefore, if anyone *is* in Christ, *he is* a new creation; old things have passed away; behold, all things have become new (2 Corinthians 5:16-17).

In the days ahead, many will be shocked at those who will sell out for greed and personal gain. Even more sinister will be the unveiling of those who have been masquerading serpent seed behind titles, positions, and pulpits. They have carefully introduced the doctrine of demons, making people prey to the prince of the power of the air.

The False Bride

Just as Christ has His Bride, even so, Satan has his lover he is preparing to come for. As part of the ultimate deception, he is currently adorning her with gold and silver and precious stones. He is wining and dining her on the blood of the saints until she becomes drunk on their blood. Satan is fulfilling her every lust.

> And the woman was arrayed in purple and scarlet color, and decked with gold and precious stones and pearls, having a

golden cup in her hand full of abominations and filthiness of her fornication: And upon her forehead was a name written, MYSTERY, BABYLON THE GREAT, THE MOTHER OF HARLOTS AND ABOMINATIONS OF THE EARTH (Revelation 17:4-5 KJV).

This is she who is the false bride of Satan, the false church who will usher in the beast to fight against the Lamb of God. When the beast comes for the scarlet woman adorned with the world's goods, the world will arise to worship. The ten pre-appointed kings so intoxicated by his trading will give their power and wealth to him to wage the final war (Daniel 7:15-27). The tares will be exposed and identified for what they really are:

> Woe to them! For they have gone in the way of Cain, have run greedily in the error of Balaam for profit, and perished in the rebellion of Korah. These are spots in your love feasts, while they feast with you without fear, serving *only* themselves. *They are* clouds without water, carried about by the winds; late autumn trees without fruit, twice dead, pulled up by the roots (Jude 11-12).

The apostle Jude agrees with Peter. The attempt of the tares to be undetected will not succeed. They will be caught, separated, bound and burned:

> But these, like natural brute beasts made to be caught and destroyed, speak evil of the things they do not understand, and will utterly perish in their own corruption, *and* will receive the wages of unrighteousness, *as* those who count it pleasure to carouse in the daytime. *They are* spots and blemishes, carousing in their own deceptions while they feast with you, having eyes full of adultery and that cannot cease from

sin, enticing unstable souls. *They have* a heart trained in covetous practices, *and are* accursed children (2 Peter 2:12-14).

The false bride of the beast will be seen by all for who she is as well, unlike the unblemished Bride. The scarlet harlot is spotted, blemished, wrinkled, and drunk. Christ will destroy her at His coming:

> His eyes were as a flame of fire, and on his head were many crowns; and he had a name written, that no man knew, but he himself.... And I saw the beast, and the kings of the earth, and their armies, gathered together to make war against him that sat on the horse, and against his army. And the beast was taken, and with him the false prophet that wrought miracles before him, with which he deceived them that had received the mark of the beast, and them that worshipped his image. These both were cast alive into a lake of fire burning with brimstone. And the remnant were slain with the sword of him that sat upon the horse, which sword proceeded out of his mouth: and all the fowls were filled with their flesh (Revelation 19:12, 19-21 KJV).

Christ Will Separate the Wheat From the Tares

As the fullness of times comes upon us, the tares of the serpent seed (Matthew 13:30, 39-41) will emerge to strengthen the deception of the coming lawless one. Scripture seems to indicate that even some born-again believers may succumb to a pseudo spirituality of elitism leading to apostasy, abandoning humility and the love of the brethren. They will go out from among us, becoming like a cancer to the church. In the days ahead, even now, we will need to discern between the wheat and the tares. Some people we will need to allow to separate from us; others we must attempt to pull from the fire.

Little children, it is the last hour; and as you have heard that the Antichrist is coming, even now many antichrists have come, by which we know that it is the last hour. They went out from us, but they were not of us; for if they had been of us, they would have continued with us; but *they went out* that they might be made manifest, that none of them were of us (1 John 2:18-19).

Keep yourselves in the love of God, looking for the mercy of our Lord Jesus Christ unto eternal life. And of some have compassion, making a difference: And others save with fear, pulling them out of the fire; hating even the garment spotted by the flesh (Jude 21-23 KJV).

Even with a casual reading of the last few chapters of Revelation, it's difficult to miss the reason Jesus saddles up His white horse. Riding forth with eyes like fire and crowned in glory, He comes to bring justice to His saints and destruction to the wicked.

The Marriage Supper of the Lamb is Coming

The motivation behind this historical ride is a wedding, His wedding. For the marriage supper of the Lamb is ready and His wife has made herself ready (see Revelation 19:7).

His wife is none other than the overcoming Church – those who have separated themselves from the lukewarm existence of the Laodicean church of the last days. Blessed are those who have purchased the gold refined by fire, the garments to cover their nakedness, and the eye salve that they might see (see Revelation 3:18)

This is the Bride who has overcome the world, the flesh, and the devil just as Christ has. These will be seated with Christ on His throne just as Christ overcame and is seated with His Father on His throne.

Jesus is coming for a glorious overcoming Bride, a Bride who is fully His – a virgin in the spirit who has been washed and kept by the Word, not having spot or wrinkle or any such thing.

The Bride Is Making Herself Ready

As the days get darker, the Church isn't to go into a survival mode, but rather a revival mode, as the Bride makes herself ready. Rightly did Hosea prophesy that in the closing days a mighty revival will come upon the people of God, the Bridal Church:

> Come, and let us return to the Lord; For He has torn, but He will heal us; He has stricken, but He will bind us up. After two days He will revive us; On the third day He will raise us up, That we may live in His sight. Let us know, Let us pursue the knowledge of the Lord. His going forth is established as the morning; He will come to us like the rain, Like the latter *and* former rain to the earth (Hosea 6:1-3).

This revival will include repentance, healing, revelation, and righteousness. The word *return*, from "Come let us return to the Lord," carries the true essence of repentance as we turn from our ways to the way of the Lord. Repentance restores one to the right way of thinking and doing things. Repentance results in restoration and renewal (Acts 3:19-21). In this revival, God will heal us, bind us up, and prepare us to live in His sight.

Full Revelation and Implementation

With such a glorious promise, Hosea exhorts us to pursue the knowledge of the Lord because His going forth has been established as the morning. This is prophetic language to describe the portal of revelation Jesus opened for us at His coming. The last generation will receive the full revelation of Scripture and walk it out to its fulfillment. As we seek out this light of revelation, our hearts and minds will be opened to the understanding of mysteries and perplexing Scriptures. That which Daniel sealed up will be made known to those who go here and there. The revelation will cause them to rejoice and shine like the sun (Daniel 12:4; Matthew 13:43).

Hosea declares He will come to us like the rain – "like the latter and former rain to the earth" (Hosea 6:3). In a study of this phrase, we discover from Joel that the spiritual meaning of rain is "teachers of righteousness" (Joel 2:23). Before Christ comes, the earth will be filled with the knowledge of His glory (Habakkuk 2:14). Just as Noah, a preacher of righteousness, preached 120 years before the flood, even so, the preaching of righteousness will be fully proclaimed again to fulfill Jesus' words, "As it was in the days of Noah" (Matthew 24:37 NIV). This teaching will come forth in the spirit and power of Elijah, preparing the world and His Bride for His coming.

Awaken To His Presence

The Lord Jesus has begun to visit His bride to awaken her just as in the Song of Solomon. He is raising up clouds in the desert (Song of Solomon 3:6), looking through the lattice (2:9-10), and leaving His fragrance on the door to our place of rest. These are subtle hints to those who are aware of His desire and presence. They discover God is not in the familiar, but rather in the marketplace (3:1-4).

Those who awaken and arise to obtain the Father's blessing will discover like Jacob that "the Lord is in this place, and I did not know *it*" (Genesis 28:16). Others will awaken to discover God speaking as He did to Peter, James, and John on the mountain of transfiguration. They fell asleep while in prayer, but when they were fully awake they saw the glory of the Lord (Luke 9:28-32). The Lord wants to fully awaken us to His glory!

Finally, like Nehemiah, God is awakening His body to the disrepair of His dwelling place. This awakening comes with a resolve to restore the broken walls and gates burned by fire (Nehemiah 1:3-4). It's time to arise, rebuild, and restore the city of God.

A Love Revolution Is Coming

Jesus said that in the last days the love of many will grow cold because "lawlessness will abound" (Matthew 24:12). We must not allow our love toward God, one another, and the truth to grow cold. It's time to fall in love with the Lord all over again. With a grateful heart, drink deeply of His Word. Ask the Holy Spirit to fill your heart with His love (Romans 5:5).

A love revolution is on the horizon. It's time to seek the welfare of others even above ourselves. We emulate Christ as we lay down our lives for others because of love. Every time I have done this thinking I'm going to miss out by putting others first, the Lord suddenly blesses me over and above what I thought I missed.

We must not only love God with everything we have, we must also love our neighbors with the same level of passion. It's time to be filled with love and invade our neighbors' space with God's goodness. Faith works through love and love is the language of miracles. Multitudes around us are in need of a miracle. Widows, orphans, single moms and dads. The sick, demonized, and impoverished are waiting for a love-filled miracle. They are waiting for Christ's disciples to look like Him and love like Him.

The Church will experience a love revolution that will define it as Christ's disciples. It is this love working through faith that will bring in the remaining harvest.

All of heaven and earth is awaiting the sound of two voices combined – the Spirit and the Bride – combined in absolute agreement and readiness. When they speak together, the Bride will have reached the fullness of preparation and the glorious conclusion of all things will come:

> "I, Jesus, have sent my angel to give you this testimony for the churches. I am the Root and the Offspring of David, and the bright Morning Star." The Spirit and the bride say, "Come!" And let him who hears say, "Come!" Whoever is thirsty, let him come; and whoever wishes, let him take the free gift of the water of life (Revelation 22:16-17 NIV).

Until that time, there are four areas of preparation for us to consider and act on in faith. This is the focus of the last chapter.

CHAPTER 10

PREPARING FOR THE DAYS AHEAD

I have attempted throughout this book to alert the body of Christ to what's coming. Multitudes in the Western church have no grid work for what is about to transpire on planet Earth. They have been lulled to sleep by a false sense of security, believing a confession of faith and a good life will somehow insulate them from the powers of darkness with no further cares. I fear for those who have dismissed the supernatural power of God being overtaken by the supernatural power of darkness.

I could have included much more in this book regarding UFOs, star gates, and other Nephilim activities that are increasing daily. There is fascinating evidence on earth regarding activities in the earth preparing it for a return of second heaven wickedness of the likes we have never experienced. It's no wonder Scripture declares that many who have no hope in God will expire for fear.

> And there shall be signs in the sun, and in the moon, and in the stars; and upon the earth distress of nations, with perplexity; the sea and the waves roaring; Men's hearts

failing them for fear, and for looking after those things which are coming on the earth: for the powers of heaven shall be shaken (Luke 21:25-26 KJV).

While this book is delightful for some, it may have been very disturbing for others – too much dark information. I pray it will serve its purpose to awaken and prepare the Bride of Christ for His coming. I pray it will save multitudes from the slippery slope of apostasy that sets in before the full-blown events the Scriptures tell us are to occur.

Coming to terms with the biblical facts regarding the last days will prepare us for the days ahead. The book of Revelation was written to inform us of those things that must take place before the revelation of Jesus Christ comes to the entire world. Becoming familiar with the book of Revelation, combined with the words of Jesus in Matthew 24 and various insights throughout the epistles, will require some time and effort, but will yield immeasurable rewards in the times to come.

Let's consider briefly four main areas of preparation.

Mental Preparation:
Set Your Minds On Things Above

To avoid the great apostasy that is coming, we must sharpen our discernment by exercising the Word of God to avoid deception and unbelief (Hebrews 5:14). However, one tendency of believers is to reduce spiritual principles into natural, logical steps. With comfort, many have taken these steps toward spiritual truths, believing they have logically connected the dots and have acquired the desired spiritual result. This deceptive practice has led to a mental ascension to truth void of spiritual reality and grace. For example, Jesus commands His disciples to cast out demons. In our minds, we say, *yes we must*, and *yes I will*, as giving compliance to the command. Yet most Christians have never cast out a demon, or if they suspected one was close, it would be avoided at all cost.

This may seem harsh, but it is a true and insightful conclusion to how Christianity has produced powerless, fearful believers. The sooner one comes to grips with the truth of a real and operational dark spiritual world intent on destroying you by any means, the sooner one will awaken to their identity in Christ. The book of Romans warns us about intellectual ascension to spiritual truths. The apostle Paul writes:

> For those who live according to the flesh set their minds on the things of the flesh, but those who live according to the Spirit, the things of the Spirit. For to be carnally minded is death, but to be spiritually minded is life and peace (Romans 8:5-6).

The principle set forth here declares that our natural mind does not, or cannot, lay hold of spiritual realities sufficiently to provide us with the life and peace they afford. These realities of spiritual truth must be received on a spiritual level that supercedes what seems contrary to the mind. Our minds receive peace as a by-product experience of study and meditation (see Isaiah 26:3).

The first place to engage your mind to prepare and understand what to do in times ahead is to follow the apostle Paul's admonishment to the Colossians:

> If then you were raised with Christ, seek those things which are above, where Christ is, sitting at the right hand of God. Set your mind on things above, not on things on the earth. For you died, and your life is hidden with Christ in God. (Colossians 3:1-3).

2 – Emotional Preparation:
As He Is, So Are We In This World

The apostle Paul assured Timothy:

For God has not given us a spirit of fear, but of power and of love and of a sound mind (2 Timothy 1:7).

The apostle John wrote these words to encourage us:

Love has been perfected among us in this: that we may have boldness in the day of judgment; because as He is, so are we in this world. There is no fear in love; but perfect love casts out fear, because fear involves torment. But he who fears has not been made perfect in love. We love Him because He first loved us (1 John 4:17-19).

Confidence in God's love toward us regardless of what we face is our comfort, our courage, and our opportunity to witness to His faithfulness. If you love somebody, you can go through anything for them to champion their cause, their message, and their life. The reality of David's confession in Psalm 27:1 is the truth the apostle John declared. David proclaimed:

The Lord *is* my light and my salvation; whom shall I fear?
The Lord *is* the strength of my life; of whom shall I be afraid?

This affirms the apostle John's statement: "As He is, so are we in this world" (1 John 4:17). Just as He, Jesus, is seated at the right hand of the Father, victorious over all the power of darkness, so are we in this world! We are victorious overcomers! These are not patronizing answers, but rather spiritual truths to be individually embraced to ensure a powerful finish in the coming days.

Natural Preparation:
Prepare Practically While Occupying and Expanding the Kingdom

Where do I get blueprints for my ark? There aren't any available. Remember, God said He wouldn't destroy the earth by a flood again. This time the judgment will be by fire, so you will need to be fireproof, spiritually speaking, for our God is a consuming fire (see Hebrews 12:29 and 2 Peter 3:10). Jesus promised to baptize us with the Holy Spirit and fire to purge us from the consumable issues of sin residing within us. This will result in us being *part* of the fire, not a victim of it (see Matthew 3:11-12).

Prudently speaking, I believe the days ahead can best be met by some very practical means:

- Having access to a reliable source of food and water is a must.

- Purposely acquire a reachable network of friends, loyal to Christ, who are willing to embrace the Acts 2:42-46 model of sharing and fellowship.

- Become debt free, and being familiar with bartering would be wise.

- Pursue basic survival skills from published and practical sources.

Personally, I do not hold to an escape mentality, with the exception of embracing the biblical fact that believers will be saved from the wrath to come (1 Thessalonians 1:9-10). Therefore, we are to carry on as normally as possible, continuing to occupy and expand the kingdom until He comes. Your preparation may vary based on when you believe the rapture will occur.

Spiritual Preparation:
Live a Holy Life, Preach Righteousness, Overcome Evil

While the previous three areas of preparation are important, they should all yield to spiritual preparation as being the most important. Noah was saved out of the antediluvian world because he was righteous (Genesis 7:1). To overlook or minimize this spiritual reality would be disastrous. Just as Noah lived among the fallen watchers and their offspring, the Nephilim, even so, we will also in the days ahead. Our response should be twofold:

1. Keep ourselves from being defiled by them doctrinally and physically.

2. Like Noah, preach righteousness and overcome wickedness to save people and prepare them for what is to come (we see this from others in Scripture, such as Abraham, Joseph, David, Joshua, and Jesus).

I am convinced that every believer needs to be thoroughly trained and mobilized just as the early disciples were. Each one ought to be proficient at healing the sick, casting out demons, and working miracles of provision. Each ought to know how to possess his or her own soul, how to interact with the holy angels, and like Jesus be able to walk through a crowd who would try to prematurely take your life. These are spiritual essentials of a practical nature that must be undergirded with a lifestyle of holiness, righteousness, and justice. I believe Christians are to be the basic providers of supernatural health care, healing the sick and staying healthy according to our inheritance in Christ Jesus. If Psalm 91 is true, which I believe it is, then God is our shield and exceedingly great reward.

I think it would do believers good to remember the symbol of our faith is the cross. The life of a disciple can be hazardous, and faith is risky. We have not been called to a life of safety, rather sacrifice for the cause of Christ. This is the right mindset for what's ahead.

If our number one priority is to win the lost and make disciples while remaining holy, we will have our priorities in order. It ought to be our goal not to just get ourselves to heaven, but also everybody else we can loose from the clutches of evil. Jesus put the conclusion of this age in these terms:

> And this gospel of the kingdom will be preached in all the world as a witness to all the nations, and then the end will come (Matthew 24:14).

Walk Out the Faith and Hope That Is In You!

The fallen watchers, the Nephilim, even Satan – they fear you, because you have authority and power over them! They will run and hide, and live life in disguise. They will be in our midst, but are not to be the center of our attention. It's time to arise and shine, for our light has come and the glory of the Lord is risen upon us! (Isaiah 60:1-2). These are not days to hide or withdraw, rather days to overcome, to walk out the faith and hope that is in us!

The best preparation for the days ahead is to have a good working faith engaged in the spiritual realities present in this world. God is going to allow us to cover the earth with the knowledge of His glory (Habakkuk 2:14).

Maranatha! Even so, Lord Jesus, come!

APPENDIX

APPENDIX A

Sixteen Strongmen

In two passages of Scripture, Jesus describes the demonic presence controlling a person as the "strongman." Scripture identifies at least sixteen strongmen and their typical manifestations. Through the ministry of the Holy Spirit, the interview process, and character observation, the prayer minister can identify what strongman may be behind the persistent problems in a person's life. Once identified, it is more readily removed and replaced with God's truth and attributes. Bind the spirit, loose its grip and operation in the person's life, and expel the spirit in Jesus' name.

1. **Spirit of Divination** – Acts 16:16-18
   a. Root: Work of the flesh (Galatians 5:19-21)
   b. Fruit: Counterfeit gifts of the Holy Spirit (Matthew 7:20; 1 Corinthians 12:9-12); Scriptural Insights (2 Corinthians 6:17; Jeremiah 27:9-10; 2 Kings 17:17; Isaiah 45:13-14; Micah 5:12; Revelation 21:8)
   c. Manifestations:
      - Fortuneteller – Psychic (Micah 5:12; Isaiah 2:6)
      - Witch or sorcerer (Exodus 22:18)
      - Rebellion (1 Samuel 15:23)
      - Horoscopes – Zodiac –Pseudoastronomy (Isaiah 47:13; Leviticus 19:26; Jeremiah 10:2)
      - Hypnotist (Deuteronomy 18:11; Isaiah 19:3)
      - Drug abuse (Galatians 5:20; Revelation 9:21; 18:23, 21:8)
      - Divination/Dowsing (Hosea 4:12)
      - Magic(k) (non-slight of hand, legerdemain) (Exodus 7:11, 8:7, 9:11)

2. **Familiar Spirit** – Leviticus 19:31
   a. Root: Work of the flesh (Galatians 5:19-21, Iniquity – Exodus 20:6)
   b. Fruit: Information and speech from demonic sources
   c. Scriptural Insights: (Leviticus 20:27; Exodus 20:5; 34:7; 1 Samuel 28:5-19; 1 Chronicles 13-14; Isaiah 8:19)
   d. Manifestations:
      - Clairvoyant or medium (1 Samuel 28:7-8; Isaiah 8:19)
      - Peeping and muttering (Isaiah 8:19, 29:4; 59:3)
      - Necromancer (Deuteronomy 18:11; 1 Chronicles 10:13)
      - Yoga (1 Timothy 4:1)
      - Passive minds (Jeremiah 23:16, 25, 32; 27:9-10)
      - False prophecy (Isaiah 29:4; Ezekiel 13:17; Revelation 2:20)

3. **Spirit of Jealousy** – Numbers 5:14
   a. Root: Work of the flesh (Galatians 5:19-21)
   b. Fruit: Deception, fear, chronic liar, no close friends, gossip
   c. Scriptural Insights: (John 8:44; Proverbs 3:25-26; 1 Timothy 4:7; 2 Peter 2:1-2)
   d. Manifestations:
      - Contentions (Proverbs 13:10)
      - Hatred (Genesis 37:3,4,8; 1 Thessalonians 4:8)
      - Strife (Proverbs 10:12)
      - Cruelty (Song of Solomon 8:6; Proverbs 27:4)
      - Anger (Genesis 4:5-6; Proverbs 6:34; 14:29, 22:24-25)
      - Murder (Genesis 4:8)
      - Revenge (Proverbs 6:34; 14:16-17)
      - Envy (Proverbs 14:30)
      - Divisions (Galatians 5:19)
      - Competition (Genesis 4:4-5)

APPENDIX A SIXTEEN STRONGMEN

4. **Lying Spirit** – 2 Chronicles 18:22
   a. Root: Work of the flesh (Galatians 5:19-21)
   b. Fruit: Deception, fear, chronic liar, no close friends, gossip
   c. Scriptural Insights (John 8:44; Proverbs 3:25-26; 1 Timothy 4:7; 2 Peter 2:1-2)
   d. Manifestations:
      - Lies (2 Chronicles 18:22; Proverbs 6:16-19)
      - Slander (Proverbs 10:18)
      - Flattery (Psalm 78:36; Proverbs 20:19; 26:28; 29:5)
      - Gossip (1 Timothy 6:20; 2 Timothy 2:16)
      - Accusations (Psalm 31:18)
      - False Prophecy (Matthew 7:15; Jeremiah 23:16-17)
      - Deception (2 Thessalonians 2:9-13)
      - Superstition (1 Timothy 4:7)
      - False teachers (2 Peter 2:1-3)

5. **Spirit of Haughtiness (Pride)** – Proverbs 16:18
   a. Root: Work of the flesh (Galatians 5:19-21)
   b. Fruit: Intractableness, self-righteousness, arrogant, contentious
   c. Scriptural Insights: (Proverbs 6:16-17; 16:18; 13:10; 1 Samuel 15:23; Ezekiel 16:45-50)
   d. Manifestations:
      - Pride (Proverbs 6:16-17; 16:18; 28:25; Isaiah 16:6)
      - Arrogance (2 Samuel 22:28; Jeremiah 48:29)
      - Scornful (Proverbs 1:22; 3:34; 21:24)
      - Strife (Proverbs 28:25)
      - Contentious (Proverbs 13:10)
      - Rebellion (1 Samuel 15:23; Proverbs 29:1)
      - Rejection (Psalm 10:4; Jeremiah 43:2)
      - Obstinate (hardheaded) (Proverbs 29:1; Daniel 5:20)

6. **Seducing Spirits** – 1 Timothy 4:1
   a. Root: Work of the flesh (Galatians 5:19)
   b. Fruit: Fascinating ways to evil, deduction, enticer, and attractions
   c. Scriptural Insights: (1 Timothy 4:1; James 1:14-15; Genesis 3:6; Mark 13:22; 2 Timothy 3:2-5, 13-15)
   d. Manifestations:
      - Addictions (Romans 8:15; 2 Peter 2:19)
      - Compulsive sin (Proverbs 5:22; John 8:34)
      - Bondage to sin (2 Timothy 2:26)
      - Fears (Romans 8:15; Hebrews 2:14-15)
      - Slave to corruption (Luke 8:26-29; Acts 8:23; Romans 6:16)

7. **Spirit of Infirmity** – Luke 13:11-13, 16
   a. Root: Man's sin and disobedience (Deuteronomy 28:15)
   b. Fruit: Lame, frail
   c. Scriptural Insights: (John 5:5; Acts 3:2; 4:9)
   d. Manifestations:
      - Asthma, allergies, hay fever (John 5:5)
      - Arthritis (John 5:5)
      - Cancer, weakness, oppression (Acts 10:38)

8. **Spirit of Heaviness** – Isaiah 61:3
   a. Root: Separation from God, immorality, idolatry, sorrow
   b. Fruit: Grief, sorrow, depression, despair
   c. Scriptural Insights: (Romans 6:16; Isaiah 53:4)
   d. Manifestations:
      - Despair, hopelessness (2 Corinthians 1:8-9)
      - Suicidal thoughts (Mark 9:22)
      - Depression (Isaiah 61:3; Genesis 37:34-35; Job 9:16-35)
      - Inner hurts (Luke 4:18; Proverbs 18:14)
      - Self pity (Psalm 69:20)
      - Grief (Proverbs 15:13)

APPENDIX A SIXTEEN STRONGMEN

9. **Spirit of Whoredom** – Hosea 5:4
    a. Root: Work of the flesh (Galatians 5:19-21)
    b. Fruit: Dissatisfaction, adultery, idolatry, excess
    c. Scriptural Insights: (Hosea 5:12; 1 Corinthians 6:13, 15, 18-20; 1 Timothy 6:7-12; Philippians 3:18-19)
    d. Manifestations:
        - Idolatry (Judges 2:17; Leviticus 17:7; Ezekiel 16:15-34)
        - Love of money (Proverbs 15:27; 1 Timothy 6:7-14)
        - Excessive appetite (1 Corinthians 6:13-16; Philippians 3:19)
        - Worldliness (James 4:4)
        - Fornication (Galatians 5:19)
        - Adultery (Ezekiel 16:15, 28)

10. **Deaf and Dumb Spirit** – Mark 9:17-29
    a. Root: Spiritual attack/demonic oppression
    b. Fruit: Seizures, mute, deafness, blindness
    c. Scriptural Insights: (Mark 9:17-29; Luke 9:42; 11:26; Matthew 12:22)
    d. Manifestations:
        - Seizures (Mark 9:18,20,26)
        - Ear problems (Mark 9:25-26)
        - Mental illness (Matthew 17:15; Mark 5:5)
        - Mute (Isaiah 35:5-6; Luke 11:14; Matthew 15:30-31)
        - Gnashing teeth (Mark 9:18)
        - Crying (Mark 9:26)
        - Drowning (Mark 9:22)

11. **Spirit of Fear** – 2 Timothy 1:7
    a. Root: Demonic oppression, trauma
    b. Fruit: Anxiety, fear, phobias, torment
    c. Scriptural Insights: (2 Timothy 1:7; Matthew 8:26; Revelation 21:8; Genesis 3:10; 1 John 4:18; Luke 21:26; Job 3:25)

d. Manifestations:
- Anxiety (1 Peter 5:7)
- Untrusting/Doubt (Matthew 8:26; Revelation 21:8)
- Fear of death (Psalm 55:4; Hebrews 2:14-15)
- Nightmares (Psalm 91:5-6; Isaiah 54:14)
- Heart attack (Luke 21:26; John 14:27)
- Phobias (Isaiah 13:7-8)

12. 2**Spirit of the Antichrist** – 1 John 4:3
    a. Root: Demonic
    b. Fruit: Unrighteousness, disrespect, injustice, lawlessness
    c. Scriptural Insights: (1 John 2:22; 4:3,6; 2 John 1:10-11)
    d. Manifestations:
       - Denies atonement (1 John 4:3)
       - Humanism (2 Thessalonians 2:3-4)
       - Heresies (1 John 2:18-19)
       - Deception (2 John 1:7)
       - Antichristian (Revelation 13:7)
       - Lawlessness (2 Thessalonians 2:3-12)

13. **Spirit of Error** – 1 John 4:6
    a. Root: Work of the flesh (Galatians 5:19-21)
    b. Fruit: Error, New Age movement and false doctrines
    c. Scriptural Insights: (1 John 4:6; 2 Peter 3:17; James 5:19-20)
    d. Manifestations:
       - Error (Proverbs 14:22; 2 Peter 3:16-17)
       - False doctrines (1 Timothy 6:20-21; Titus 3:10; 1 John 4:1-6)
       - New Age movement (2 Peter 2:10)
       - Defensive/Argumentative
       - Unteachable (Proverbs 10:17; 2 Timothy 4:1-4)
       - Unsubmissive (Proverbs 29)

14. **Spirit of Death** – John 8:44
    a. Root: Demonic oppression to remove life
    b. Fruit: Accidents, life-taking sickness, disease, suicide

APPENDIX A SIXTEEN STRONGMEN

    c. Scriptural Insights: (John 8:44; Ezekiel 12:23; 1 Corinthians 10:10)
    d. Manifestations:
- Suicidal
- Depression
- Anxiety

15. **Perverse Spirit** – Isaiah 19:14
    a. Root: Work of the flesh (Galatians 5:19-21)
    b. Fruit: Sexual sins, filthiness, abuse
    c. Scriptural Insights: (Isaiah 19:14; Romans 1:26-28; Isaiah 5:20)
    d. Manifestations:
       - Worry (Proverbs 19:3)
       - Twisting the word (Acts 13:10; 2 Peter 2:14)
       - Doctrinal error (Isaiah 19:14; Romans 1:22-23)
       - Abortion (Exodus 21:22-25)
       - Filthiness (Proverbs 2:12; 23:33)
       - Sexual perversion (Romans 1:17-32; 2 Timothy 3:2)
       - Atheist (Proverbs 14:2; Romans 1:30)
       - Foolishness (Proverbs 1:22; 19:1)
       - Child abuse, incest, pornography, broken spirit, etc.

16. **The Spirit of Bondage** – Romans 8:15; Galatians 5:1
    a. Root: Work of the flesh – Galatians 5:19-21
    b. Fruit: Imprisonment to the devil, addictions, fear, dishonesty
    c. Scriptural Insights: (2 Peter 2:19; Proverbs 5:22; John 8:34; 2 Timothy 2:26; Romans 6:16; 7:23; 8:15; Luke 8:26-29; Acts 8:23)
    d. Manifestations:
       - Captivity to the devil
       - Compulsive sin
       - Bondage to sin
       - Addictions
       - Fear of death
       - Slave of corruption

APPENDIX B

PROFILE OF A FALSE PROPHET AND OTHER FALSE MINISTRIES AND MINISTERS

There are many signs that reveal a false prophet or minister claiming to be operating in, or speaking by, the Spirit of God. These often parallel the many signs that expose cults and the occult. The exhortation of the apostle John was, "Beloved, do not believe every spirit, but test the spirits, whether they are of God; because many false prophets have gone out into the world" (1 John 4:1).

1. **Jesus said,** "Beware of false prophets, who come to you in sheep's clothing, but inwardly are ravenous wolves. You will know them by their fruits" (Matthew 7:15-16).

   Fruits are their works, their character, words, and deeds. Jesus tells us the false prophet will come from among us (1 John 2:19), and even remain among us (2 Peter 2:1), as they are cloaked in sheep's clothing.

   a. They look like sheep.
   b. They act like sheep.
   c. They sound like sheep.
   d. They go where sheep go.
   e. They do what sheep do.
   f. But! They speak empty words (Chaff – Jeremiah 23:28), full of deceit. Chaff is the covering shell of the wheat, so without close inspection, it could deceive one as full and true. False prophets are ravenous wolves who cause division and offenses contrary to the doctrine you have learned. They lay in wait to deceive. (see Romans 16:17-18)

APPENDIX B PROFILE OF A FALSE MINISTER

2. **Test their fruit by comparing it to the fruit of the Holy Spirit.**
   "The fruit of the Spirit is love, joy, peace, longsuffering, kindness, goodness, faithfulness, gentleness, self-control. Against such there is no law" (Galatians 5:22-23).

3. **All fruit isn't what it may seem.**
   "For false christs and false prophets will rise and show great signs and wonders to deceive, if possible, even the elect" (Matthew 24:24).

   a. They will draw you into esoteric places with great claims. But you will only find death.
   b. They will display great signs and wonders, but they will be worked by the spirit of the antichrist and demons. (Revelation 16:13-14)
   c. The devil can appear as an angel of light. (2 Corinthians 11:14)
   d. A servant is not greater than his master. (John 15:20)
   e. False prophets do many things in Jesus' name, but really don't know Him, and they practice lawlessness. (Matthew 7:21-23)

4. **False prophets will not confess full forgiveness, the incarnation, or the return of Christ as King of Kings and Lord of Lords.** (1 John 1:10; 4:2-3; 2 John 1:7)

   a. False prophets will not confess the blood of Christ is needed or even sufficient to cleanse one of their sin and unrighteousness. (1 John 1:9-10)
   b. False prophets deny Christ as both human and divine, in that He was with God in the beginning (John 1:1). He was born as a human, lived, died, and rose again as a human. (John 1:14; Luke 1:31, 24:25-26; Acts 1:9-11)

c. False prophets will not confess Christ will return as King of Kings (2 John 1:7). Jesus Himself declared: "'I am the Alpha and the Omega, *the* Beginning and *the* End,' says the Lord, 'who is and who was and who is to come, the Almighty.'" (Revelation 1:8)

5. **All men speak well of him.**
   "For so did their fathers to the false prophets." (Luke 6:26)

   a. False prophets speak smooth and flattering words. (Romans 16:18)
   b. False prophets say to those who despise the Lord and follow the dictates of their own hearts, "The Lord says you shall have peace," and "No evil shall come upon you." (Jeremiah 23:17)
   c. The world will hear him. (1 John 4:5-6)
   d. The world will not hate him. (John 15:18-19)

6. **Full of deceit and fraud.** (Acts 13:6-10)
   Opposes those who bring truth and expose their identity. (Acts 13:6-12)

7. **Carries the secret motive of material and financial gain.** (2 Corinthians 11:5-15)
   True ministers minister regardless of cost or gain, being sent out by the Lord.

8. **Hiding shameful things.** (2 Corinthians 4:1-2)
   a. Not renouncing hidden things of shame.
   b. Walking in craftiness.
   c. Handling the word of God deceitfully.

9. **Takes away your liberty.** (Galatians 2:4; 3:1-3)
   a. Compels you to do works. (Galatians 2:1-5; 1 Corinthians 7:18-19)
   b. Forbids you to marry or eat certain foods. (1 Timothy 4:3)

APPENDIX B PROFILE OF A FALSE MINISTER

10. "Secretly bring in destructive heresies, even denying the Lord who bought them, and bring on themselves swift destruction." (2 Peter 2:1-23)

    a. Operates in the beginning secretly, works with individuals or in small groups without accountability. Avoids testing or correction.
    b. Follows destructive ways.
    c. Blasphemes the way of truth.
    d. By covetousness, exploits with deceptive words.
    e. Walks according to the flesh in the lust of uncleanness.
    f. Despises authority.
    g. Presumptuous, self-willed, speaks evil of dignitaries, church leaders, movements.
    h. Speaks evil things they do not understand (1 Timothy 1:3-7).
    i. They are spots and blemishes among you.
    j. Eyes full of adultery that cannot cease from sin.
    k. Entice unstable souls. Prophecy becomes the means to determine the will of God.
    l. Hearts trained in covetousness practices.
    m. Forsakes the right way.
    n. Follows the way of Balaam. Prophesies for money and fame.
    o. Madness. (Numbers 22-24)
    p. Wells without water.
    q. Clouds carried by a tempest. Weighs their words more than Scripture.
    r. Speak great swelling words of emptiness.
    s. Prey on Christians, alluring through the lusts of the flesh and lewdness.
    t. Promise liberty, while they are enslaved to corruption.
    u. Like a dog that returns to his own vomit.
    v. A sow, having washed, returns to her wallow in the mire.
    w. They themselves were once a believer, now apostate.

x. They see visions, dream and prophesy by a false spirit. (Jeremiah 23:13)
y. They lord it over people, overcome them and bring them into bondage.
z. Their activity and operation will increase as the tolerance for unbiblical doctrine increases. (2 Timothy 4:3-4; 2 Peter 2:1-2)

In summary:

"Do not quench the Spirit. Do not despise prophecies. Test all things; hold fast what is good. Abstain from every form of evil" (1 Thessalonians 5:19-22).

"Do not fall away in the time of testing" (Luke 8:13).

APPENDIX C

THE NAMES OF NEPHILIM AFTER THE FLOOD

http://www.thewatcher.co.uk/id/giants.htm 9/4/2009
[TheWatcher.co.uk] – God does exist. Pages 4 and 5 of 5
© 1999 No copyright. Ephesians 1:17
(Note: Edited minimally for clarity)

The angels did not waste any time after the flood. They went back to work trying to spoil the line of Adam. God in His wisdom knew this and separated the offspring by their looks and gave them, no doubt, a warring nature, one that would be their downfall. We know they existed after the flood as before from various Scriptures, which we will see shortly.

It would be true to say we have not seen or heard of any recently, but that is not to say God has stopped them; it might merely be the plan of Lucifer to bide his time. Who knows, though, maybe these alien creatures we are told exist are another form of angelic children.

It is true to say during biblical times they existed, but Scripture uses other names to describe these degraded fallen angels and their descendants after the flood, in addition to the word Nephilim. They are:

Anakim – Race of giants, descendants of Nephilim.

> And there we saw the giants, the sons of Anak, which come of the giants; and we were in our own sight as grasshoppers, and so we were in their sight (Numbers 13:33).

Emim – the proud deserters, terrors, race of giants. (Genesis 14:5; Deuteronomy 2:11)

> Which also were accounted giants, as the Anakims; but the Moabites call them Emims (Deuteronomy 2:11).

Zamzummims – the evil plotters.

(That also was accounted a land of giants: giants dwelt therein in in old time; and the Ammonites call them Zamzummims (Deuteronomy 2:20).

Zuphim – watchers, angels who descended, distinct from "holy watchers" aligned with God (Numbers 23).

Sepharim – "the many…"

Zuzim – the evil ones, roaming things. (Genesis 14:5)

Rephaim from the root *rapha* = spirits, shades.

And in the fourteenth came Chedorlaomer, and the kings that were with him, and smote the Rephaims in Ashteroth Karnaim, and the Zuzims in Ham, and the Emins in Shaveh Kiriathaim (Genesis 14:5).

The book of the Jubilees remarks that Jared or Yeh-red, an Old Testament patriarch, was so called because in his days the angels descended upon the earth – Yaw-rad, which means "descend." It is interesting to note that *Jordan* comes from that same root denoting "descent, coming down, or falling" – Yar-dane, which means "the place of the descent." Jordan, "place of the descent," is located in the ancient boundary of Israel. Israel is currently a major location for sightings, and the fallen angels in disguise as "aliens."

The *Book of Enoch* explains that the Sons of God descended first onto the mountain called Hermon, which in Hebrew means "desolation," in the land of Jordan the place of the descent. Desolation is exactly what the rebel angels intended to make the earth by destroying the descendants of Adam. Obviously, to make desolate the earth, not only of man but also of God's influence, has been Satan's goal from the beginning.

One reason I think we don't see [Nephilim] today is probably God's hand over the earth, which may change after the rapture. As to the fate of the giants in biblical time we have one clue in Deuteronomy 3:11:

APPENDIX C NAMES OF NEPHILIM AFTER THE FLOOD

> For only Og king of Bashan remained of the remnant of giants; behold, his bedstead was a bedstead of iron; is it not in Rabbath of the children of Ammon? Nine cubits was the length thereof, and four cubits the breadth of it, after the cubit of a man.

Og = "long-necked." The Amorite king of Bashan was one of the last representatives of the giants of Rephaim.

Here, along with the Scriptures above, are some accounts of battles with the giants, in some cases resulting in their extinction.

Deuteronomy 31:4:

> And the Lord shall do unto them as he did to Sihon and to Og, kings of the Amorites, and unto the land of them, whom he destroyed.

Joshua 2:10:

> For we have heard how the Lord dried up the water of the Red sea for you, when ye came out of Egypt; and what ye did unto the two kings of the Amorites, that were on the other side Jordan, Sihon and Og, whom ye utterly destroyed.

Joshua 13:12:

> All the kingdom of Og in Bashan, which reigned in Ashtaroth and in Edrei, who remained of the remnant of the giants: for these did Moses smite, and cast them out.

As we can see, they were in abundance but God slowly destroyed them and gave most of their land to Israel. However, I am sure they will return when the time is right. Who knows ... maybe the antichrist will come from the line of the fallen angels.

For more information about Randy DeMain and his ministry, Kingdom Revelation, or to invite him to minister in your area, visit his website at www.kingdomrevelation.org

XPpublishing.com
A ministry of Christian Services Association